Cambridge

Elements in Business Strategy
edited by
J.-C. Spender
Kozminski University

STRATEGY-IN-PRACTICES

A Process-Philosophical Perspective on Strategy-Making

Robert C. H. Chia
University of Glasgow

David Mackay
University of Strathclyde

CAMBRIDGE
UNIVERSITY PRESS

Shaftesbury Road, Cambridge CB2 8EA, United Kingdom

One Liberty Plaza, 20th Floor, New York, NY 10006, USA

477 Williamstown Road, Port Melbourne, VIC 3207, Australia

314–321, 3rd Floor, Plot 3, Splendor Forum, Jasola District Centre,
New Delhi – 110025, India

103 Penang Road, #05–06/07, Visioncrest Commercial, Singapore 238467

Cambridge University Press is part of Cambridge University Press & Assessment,
a department of the University of Cambridge.

We share the University's mission to contribute to society through the pursuit of
education, learning and research at the highest international levels of excellence.

www.cambridge.org
Information on this title: www.cambridge.org/9781009096485

DOI: 10.1017/9781009099592

First published 2023

A catalogue record for this publication is available from the British Library.

ISBN 978-1-009-09648-5 Paperback
ISSN 2515-0693 (online)
ISSN 2515-0685 (print)

Strategy-in-Practices

A Process-Philosophical Perspective on Strategy-Making

Elements in Business Strategy

DOI: 10.1017/9781009099592
First published online: March 2023

Robert C. H. Chia
University of Glasgow

David Mackay
University of Strathclyde

Author for correspondence: David Mackay, david.mackay@strath.ac.uk

Abstract: This Element maintains that increasing strategic effectiveness involves paying greater attention to the idiosyncratic capabilities and know-how already accumulated in an organisation's shared practices and the *modus operandi* contained therein. An organisation's modus operandi describes the practiced patterned regularities that enable it to achieve a consistency of response in strategic circumstances even in the absence of any clear, formalised strategic plan. This patterned regularity known as *Strategy-in-Practices* (SiP) draws attention to the tacit influence of an organisation's shared practices on its formal strategy-making efforts. It emphasises the need for both these to be aligned so that the organisation is better prepared to cope with the challenges and opportunities it faces.

This Element also has a video abstract: www.cambridge.org/Strategy-In-Practices_ Chia/Mackay_abstract

Keywords: process philosophy, strategy, strategic change, dynamic capabilities, practices

ISBNs: 9781009096485 (PB), 9781009099592 (OC)
ISSNs: 2515-0693 (online), 2515-0685 (print)

Contents

Preface

'Strategy' is a much-vaunted term often associated with successful accomplishments in a wide range of human endeavours from our personal lives to business, politics, warfare, sports and beyond. In the world of business, strategy-making is typically associated with major decisions taken by senior management, aimed at outwitting the competition through superior intellectual assessments and well-thought-out manoeuvres. The concept of strategy, therefore, offers a useful way of rationalising causal links between innate desires, the articulated organisational goals of top management and measurable performance outcomes.

This view of strategy-making as a deliberate, top-down, goal-setting activity is widely held in practitioner and academic circles. Consequently, much of strategy research focuses its attention on the formalised efforts and outputs of CEOs and senior management, reinforcing the image of strategy-making as essentially a top-management activity oftentimes requiring individual 'heroic' interventions. This widespread view underestimates the powerful influence of broader sociocultural tendencies and everyday operational coping practices on an organisation's strategising process and creates potential strategic misalignment between aspirations and internalised capabilities and predispositions.

Consequently, a common experience among practitioner circles is that well-formulated strategic plans frequently do not deliver intended outcomes when they encounter the cut and thrust of strategic and operational realities. The typical reaction among practitioners and strategy scholars, however, is to justify ever more sophisticated ways of formulating and designing comprehensive and prescient plans for delivering executive vision, often to no greater avail. In this Element, we maintain that increasing strategic effectiveness involves paying greater attention to the idiosyncratic capabilities, practical know-how and tendencies already accumulated in an organisation's shared practices and the modus operandi contained therein.

These organisational practices themselves comprise congealed aggregations of a multitude of in situ everyday coping actions taken, throughout the history of the organisation's existence, to deal with exigencies faced over time. Because of a lack of explicit recognition, the effect of this accumulated practical know-how in tacitly shaping the more formalised strategy-making processes, and hence affecting what is considered organisationally doable, has not been fully explored. We argue here that an organisation's strategy-making efforts are unavoidably affected by broader sociocultural tendencies as well as the practical wisdom accumulated in its operational coping practices. Together they shape an organisation's modus operandi predisposing it towards a patterned consistency in its responses to strategic circumstances even in the absence of any clear, formalised strategy. This patterned regularity in an organisation's responses is what we mean by Strategy-in-Practices (SiP).

Strategy-in-Practices draws attention to the tacit and often unacknowledged capabilities contained in an organisation's shared practices and the influence these have on its formal strategy-making efforts. It points to the need for both the tacit and the explicit to be aligned so that the organisation is better prepared to cope with the challenges and opportunities it faces. In effect, modus operandi is the generative source of adaptability, nimbleness and organisational resilience that enables an organisation to cope with unstable and challenging environmental conditions. It underpins the successful strategic changes needed to assure beneficial outcomes in such changing environmental circumstances.

Underpinned by a *process* worldview, our exposition of SiP is intended to help practitioners and strategy scholars better understand how extended close-quarter engagement with the environment guided by organisational practices and operational expertise can help an organisation develop and align its capabilities with its aspirations to achieve optimal outcomes with minimum effort in a world perpetually in flux.

Introduction

> In each age of the world ... there is a general form of the forms of thought (that) like the air we breathe ... is so translucent, and so pervading, and so seemingly necessary, that only by extreme effort can we become aware of it
>
> Whitehead (1933: 20–1).

To set the scene for our exploration of Strategy-in-Practices (SiP), in this opening section we address:

- The problems arising in practice from the top-down view of strategy as a deliberate and intentional activity involving goal-setting, planning and systematic execution.
- The impact of historical and sociocultural conditioning of strategic outlooks on organisational strategy-making.
- The overlooked strategic value of operational coping practices arising spontaneously in organisations through creative, in situ responses to environmental demands, and the importance of these practices for organisational strategising.

Strategy has become a key concept in explaining organisational success. Understood in its most generic sense, strategy is fundamentally about advantage-gaining moves: seeking out and creating possibilities, grasping opportunities and exercising control over an organisation's circumstances and hence actively shaping its destiny. Within the strategy literature, it is widely assumed that success and superior long-term performance is the result of well-thought-out strategic plans. There is an abiding belief that, above and beyond the grind of daily operations, strategy is what unifies and directs organisational efforts towards these sought-after outcomes. Such established views of strategy-making speak to an unflinching faith in the ability to survive, grow and succeed through deliberate goal-setting, planning and systematic execution. Consequently, as commonly used, strategy provides a convenient way of rationalising the causal links between competitive pressures, commissioned initiatives, resource usage and shared goals.

Much of the current strategy literature examining differential organisational performances is underpinned by a philosophically *substantialist* worldview. A substantialist worldview privileges the identity, status and autonomy of individuals and entities, such as CEOs or market leading firms, and assumes that with sufficient purposeful planning involving deliberate choice and will-power, target outcomes can be achieved regardless of prevailing external circumstances. This substantialist worldview is a historical legacy passing from Parmenides in the fifth century BC through to Aristotle, Newtonian physics and beyond. Substantialism views all of reality as comprising *substances* – discrete, stable and identifiable entities that readily lend themselves to linguistic representation, logical analysis and cause and effect explanations. It is a legacy still dominant in the physical as well as the social sciences.

In much of the social sciences and especially in strategy theorising, these widespread substantialist assumptions have resulted in the privileging of:

- the discrete, autonomous, wilful individual over the shared collective
- a belief in the adequacy and accuracy of linguistic representations
- thought over action
- a reliance on the intellect rather than on the senses as the primary basis of knowing
- detached, systematic and logical analysis over in situ coping responsiveness
- deliberate, top-down, planned strategy as the basis of organisational success.

Within strategy theorising, the substantialist worldview manifests itself in the assumptions that logical analysis, deliberate rational choice and systematic goal-setting necessarily precede effective action (i.e. 'To succeed, you must have a clear strategy'). This effectively means focusing on prominent individuals – CEOs, strategy directors and so on – making individual autonomous choices, within social entities called 'organisations', that then coalesce into strategic plans that subsequently guide strategy implementation. Grounded in substantialist thinking, this formulaic approach to strategy-making has become ubiquitous among business consultants and strategy practitioners.

This view endures despite the fact that, time and again, such top-down planned approaches to strategy have been shown to be ineffective in practice. In multiple arenas, the practitioner world has experienced how well-intended elaborate plans often go awry in the face of unexpected real-world changes. As the Scottish poet Robert Burns (1786) famously noted: 'the best laid schemes o' mice an' men / Gang aft a-gley' (the finest-crafted plans often don't work out as intended). Elaborate strategic plans may look good on paper, but in practice, they are often ineffective or unhelpful in the face of unexpected environmental changes. Yet, despite this commonly recurring experience, organisational leaders continue to insist on the need for such abstract goal-setting and planning as the primary basis for strategic action.

At the root of the rational strategic planning approach are three interrelated substantialist assumptions. Firstly, an unalloyed belief in the autonomy of individual choice. Second, an assumption that cognitive representations, including linguistic representations, accurately reflect the reality of actual goings-on in the world. Third, an unchallenged belief that logical thinking and systematic analysis must always precede effective action. Methodological individualism (von Mises, 1949/1998; MacKay et al., 2021), a representationalist epistemology (Aristotle, 1998) and the privileging of thought over action (March, 1972) underpin much of contemporary strategy theorising.

In particular, the notion that thought necessarily precedes effective action is inspired by the *Cartesian* split between the mental and the physical realms (famously expressed as *cogito, ergo sum* – 'I think, therefore I am'). In this tradition, 'proper knowledge' entails cognitively representing the world around us in the form of processed mental images and linguistic concepts. The ability of language to cognitively provide an accurate picture of the situation faced as the basis for proper action is taken for granted in much of academic scholarship. Strategic action is thus explained through recourse to the meaning and intention of significant actors, and a means–ends logic of action is used to explain outcomes. March (1972: 419) describes this substantialist rationale succinctly: 'thinking should precede action ... action should serve a purpose ... (and) purpose should be defined in terms of a consistent set of pre-existent goals ... choice should be based on a consistent theory of the relation between action and its consequences'.

Within the logic of this substantialist worldview, many have come to accept the need for deliberate strategic planning as a prerequisite for ensuring organisational success. However, our reality frequently does not end up as planned simply because the world is often chaotic, unordered and perpetually changing, and planned actions take place in vastly different circumstances from those in which they were originally formulated. From lived experience, we know that rationalised expectations repeatedly fail to match up to, or even sometimes contradict, what happens in practice (Dreyfus, 1991; Chia and Holt, 2009; MacKay et al., 2021). In reality, our daily experiences suggest that spontaneous resourcefulness is oftentimes more critical than well-laid plans when attempting to successfully negotiate the vagaries of real-world challenges (Scott, 1998).

When facing dynamic or turbulent environments, there is more value in organisational coping capacities that enable members to respond 'on the hoof' than there is in pre-established plans. Such capabilities and spontaneous respon- siveness are grounded in acquired sociocultural predispositions coupled with a refined sensitivity to prevalent environmental conditions. Such contextual forces affect how individuals cope with and respond to the exigencies faced. In situ coping actions and decisions, often taken spontaneously in an unplanned way, can nevertheless inadvertently aggregate into a coherent and effective strategy over time (Mintzberg and Waters, 1985; Chia and Holt, 2009). Yet, such aggregated coping responses containing patterned regularities are often overlooked in formal strategy-making practice and research. Such omissions diminish our capacity to explain organisational success beyond widely accepted narratives extolling the virtues of a deliberate, top-down strategic planning approach.

This critique applies to some extent to Mintzberg and Waters's (1985) idea of 'emergent strategy' arising from the stream of actions and decisions made. Whilst Mintzberg and colleagues offer valuable insights about the inadvertent nature of such strategic outcomes, their work, nevertheless, remains focused on the autonomous actions and decisions of important individuals such as top managers and CEOs. Two crucial aspects of how strategy emergence necessar- ily relates to context are overlooked in the emergent strategy literature.

Firstly, the notion that strategy practitioners are autonomous individuals making deliberate choices of their own volition omits the fundamentally social nature of humans as belonging to a larger collective. As social beings, practi- tioners' worldviews, their habits and predispositions are ineluctably shaped by historical traditions, acquired sociocultural practices and inherited paradigms of comprehension. What strategy practitioners think and how they act are invari- ably shaped by broader sociocultural circumstances and conditionings. To paraphrase Karl Marx in his *Eighteenth Brumaire of Louis Bonaparte*, 'men (sic) make strategies, but they do not do so in social circumstances of their own making'. Top managers such as CEOs may like to believe that the strategic choices they make reflect their personal values, intentions and preferences, but the reality is that they are always already shaped by inherited sociocultural traditions, practices and norms. They have been socially conditioned to act, think and respond in ways that broadly conform to wider societal expectations. An organisation's approach to strategising, therefore, does not happen in isolation; it is inevitably shaped by such broader sociocultural outlooks, preferences and predispositions (MacKay et al., 2021).

For example, consider varying views of using mergers and acquisitions (M&A) as a means for expanding market reach. As a type of purposeful strategic initiative, M&A is more prevalent in some Western cultures than others, and is almost non-existent in non-Western cultures like Japan. This preference for market capture/expansion or consolidation through M&A reflects inherited sociocultural tendencies and preferences more than is currently acknowledged. Strategic initiatives that work in one culture may be resisted in a different context because they go against the grain of what is locally expected or acceptable (MacKay et al., 2021). Strategic tendencies are inextricably tied to a culture's practices and modus operandi: the collectively shared and approved ways of doing things to achieve a desired outcome. To understand why an organisation arrives at a preferred strategy, therefore, it is necessary to examine its broader sociocultural context and the inherited societal preferences and historical tendencies impacting those involved in the life of the organisation. The case of Natura, a Brazilian-headquartered multinational, helps illustrate the influence of sociocultural norms and preferences on strategy and strategy-making.

ILLUSTRATIVE EXAMPLE: NATURA, THE AMAZON AND SUSTAINABLE PRACTICE

Mackay et al. (2023) and Jones (2012) examine Natura as an example of an organisation that has thrived by developing in harmony with the social, natural and environmental context in which it is embedded.

Founded in 1969 in a small lab and shop in São Paulo, Natura Cosméticos SA is a Brazilian multinational enterprise serving beauty care markets. The name Natura – Portuguese for Nature – reflects the organisation's origin in Brazil, two-fifths of which is covered by the Amazon rain forest. Since inception, Natura has prioritised harmonious relationships with the environment and the Indigenous people of the Amazon. This attitude is reflected in a recent commitment to create 100 per cent carbon-neutral products from many recyclable materials, and use wherever possible raw materials gathered through sustainable methods from the virgin forests. Natura uses the rainforest's biodiversity as its technological platform for the research and development of its products in contrast to the mainly laboratory-based methods of its competitors. To sustainably draw from the rainforest's resources whilst guarding against 'biopiracy' – the unethical commercialisation of the region's genetic and cultural heritage – Natura entered into agreements with many thousands of small local suppliers for its raw materials. This way of operating positions the company as an empathic, locally embedded player in the market for natural cosmetics and skincare.

Natura has also nurtured a distinctive social character by operating in a way that mirrors the community-oriented culture and predispositions of the Indigenous people of the Amazon. Deprioritising corporate sales channels for its products, Natura relies on an extensive network of direct sales personnel, numbering over 1.4 million as of 2022. It supports capability development in daily operations, including investing in the skills of door-to-door associates, providing them payment machines and internet selling infrastructure. These acts support many local jobs whilst nurturing brand evangelists and rich flows of communication with the consumer base all across Brazil. This commitment to shared prosperity with Brazilian communities, including continued investment in local education and employment initiatives, imbues Natura with a competitive advantage over those acting in a less-attuned way to local culture and norms.

And bucking a previous industry trend, Natura has focused development on cosmetic products that meet consumer wellness needs, prioritising health over beauty in its marketing messages. This move was in alignment with broader national attitudes in Brazil and customer insights flowing from its direct sales network. Over the years, Brazilian consumers have responded by rewarding Natura with market share (e.g. a 43 per cent compound annual rate of revenue growth from 1979 to 1989). In recent decades, global attitudes have shifted towards this natural approach. As a result, Natura has emerged as an authentic and credible proponent of wellness with consumers around the world. This advantage has enabled Natura to actively expand into overseas markets, and to acquire firms such as Avon and the Body Shop (that once would have been considered giants in comparison to Natura). An emergent strategy that was initiated by local tendencies, and shaped by immediate sociocultural influences, has unexpectedly found resonance with global sentiments.

Secondly, strategic activity is inseparable from everyday operational activities and so-called tactical responses in a way that is seldom acknowledged in strategy theory. In practice, where the operational ends and where the strategic begins is unclear and subject to differing opinions (Mackay and Zundel, 2017). The widely accepted distinction between the 'operational' and the 'strategic' is, in truth, arbitrary and any imagined separation is more a result of the influence of widely disseminated business school teaching and consultancy practices grounded in the convenience of a discipline-based teaching curriculum.

In practice, there are no obvious dividing lines or convenient distinctions for easily separating activities in an organisation. For example, are the spontaneous coping actions of a cabin crew member calming a distraught passenger on a turbulent flight simply an operational matter or a matter of strategic consequence? One could argue this action is clearly an operational matter, until it is recorded and shared on social media, with a positive impact on airline reputation and share price. What may seem innocuous can in fact be the genesis of organisational-level 'strategic' consequences. Every apparently mundane but effective coping or creative action has the potential for a 'trickle up' effect on strategic outcomes. But an emphasis on top-down strategy-making often blinds us to the humble operational beginnings of many 'strategic' initiatives.

ILLUSTRATIVE EXAMPLE: THE STRATEGIC VALUE OF TAP-TONE CHECKS

In the early 1980s one of the authors was involved in the management of a can-manufacturing plant in the Asia-Pacific region serving clients in the breweries and beverage industries. To ensure product integrity and prevent leakage, a lacquer coating is sprayed inside each can at a rate of 300 cans per minute. Issues with this physical process and the possibility of leaking cans are always a concern when manufacturing at such high speeds. If not detected, costly reputational damage can arise from a customer receiving defective leaking cans. On one such occasion, a Japanese soft drinks customer complained of leaking cans and threatened to withdraw their business unless there was a more stringent quality check of the millions of cans supplied to them monthly.

In this instance, the threat of losing a much-valued business customer led to the author consulting the production team about whether it was possible to do a quality check that was cost-effective and not overly labour intensive. To his surprise he was told it might actually be possible to do so without too much hassle! The operators were already required to inspect the cans for external printing defects and this was done after the cans were washed, dried and inverted onto a moving conveyor belt for the final visual inspection. It was an onerous task since they were required at their station to visually check the over 300,000 cans produced during each eight-hour shift. To alleviate themselves of their boredom from this routine, they would occasionally use fashioned wooden sticks to tap on the bases of the cans to create some rhythm and music to entertain themselves as they worked. From this improvised practice they came to notice that occasionally some cans made a different flat sound when tapped compared to others. On further investigation, it turned out that the cause of this flat sound was that the lacquer had not been properly sprayed, meaning the internal surfaces were not evenly coated and so were more likely to leak when filled.

An experienced operator pointed out that it was possible to tell if a can was liable to leak simply by listening to the tone it emitted when tapped. This piece of practical wisdom arising from operational experience proved a vital spark in identifying how to quickly pick up the defective ones before they were sent off. A 'tap-tone' check was instituted based on this operational insight, addressing the immediate client concerns and eventually giving the firm a significant strategic advantage over its competitors in terms of customer quality assurance and wastage cost reduction outcomes.

Over time, this 'tap-tone' check was introduced to all the multinational's subsidiary operations worldwide. A seemingly small and innocuous difference of sound detected through the carrying out of mundane operational tasks ended up providing a crucial strategic advantage for the firm. This and many other examples illustrate how strategy can emerge inadvertently from the bowels of everyday operations.

Strategising – the enactment of activity relating to strategy-making – does not take place in a vacuum but rather in the context of everyday goings-on within and around an organisation (Mackay et al., 2023). Taking cognizance of the influence of context, those involved in strategising may supplement abstract strategy analysis with practical insights into the possibilities and limitations of resources, capabilities, internalised predispositions and practices. The perceived plausibility of an organisation's strategy will be impacted by the extent to which it aligns with its accumulated practical expertise and established operational capabilities. Awareness of accrued, distinctive aspects of an organisation – the '*differences which make a difference*' (Bateson, 1972: 453, emphasis original) – can make the difference between success and failure in strategic outcomes. Effective coping and advantage-seeking impulses naturally arising from an organisational modus operandi can result in strategic coherence even in the absence of an explicit strategic plan. Operational know-how often serves as a source of consistency and patterned regularity that can influence an organisation's strategising activities.

These two influences on organisational strategy-making – the historical and sociocultural conditioning of strategic tendencies, outlooks and predispositions and the impact of effective operational coping capabilities on strategising – constitute the primary focus of this Element. These contextual factors play a critical role in shaping strategy-making in organisational life under the umbrella of SiP.

1 Why Strategy-in-Practices?

Rather than assuming that all firms must have a strategy, it may be necessary to ask: Why is there no strategy here? What are the characteristics of the strategy-less organization?

Inkpen and Choudhury (1995: 313)

In this section, we:

- Challenge the dominant view that strategic planning is vital for ensuring long-term performance gains and examine the alternative 'emergent' strategy approach.
- Articulate a distinction between *purposive* and *purposeful* action and show how the former intimates a modus operandi – a consistent patterned responsiveness arising from shared practices – as the originating source of emergent strategy.
- Explain how SiP defines an alternative approach in which strategy-making reflects and is reflected in the organisational modus operandi.
- Examine the role and value of *mêtis*, a form of practical intelligence, in ongoing coping and strategising efforts in an organisation.

In our introductory section we pointed out that it is widely believed that organisations succeed primarily when top management practitioners, relying on rational thinking and systematic analysis, develop elaborate strategic plans that are then implemented to produce desired measurable outcomes (Porter, 1980; Johnson and Scholes, 1997). The conventional wisdom is that without such prior purposeful setting of strategic objectives and the detailed planning of various corresponding initiatives for intervention, organisational efforts will be random and ineffective – 'if you don't know where you are going, any road will take you there'. When strategic planning is understood as an imperative, organisational activity is framed in terms of the 'anticipations, incentives, and desires' of those making decisions and setting goals (March, 2003: 205). But what if this wholesale commitment to a rational and systematic approach is flawed? And what if strategic potential actually resides not so much in articulated strategic plans but in the multitude of tacit, spontaneous coping actions taken by organisational members in dealing with situational exigencies?

This questioning of the need for a formally articulated strategic plan for an organisation to succeed isn't new. In a provocative *Strategic Management Journal* paper, Inkpen and Choudhury (1995) noted that while strategy researchers normally expected to find such articulated strategies in their investigations of successful organisations, this was not always the case. They described being baffled by some apparently 'strategy-less' yet successful organisations they encountered; those without any evidence of any deliberate, pre-formulated strategy already in place. In attempting to explain this apparent absence of an explicitly articulated strategy, Inkpen and Choudhury noted approvingly Mintzberg's (1978) observation that strategy sometimes 'emerges' as a 'pattern in a stream of decisions' instead of pre-existing as an explicitly formulated plan. They used this notion of 'emergent strategy' to explain why some organisations might appear 'strategy-less'.

But Inkpen and Choudhury (1995) did not explore how an 'emergent strategy' was possible at all, nor did Mintzberg and his colleagues (Mintzberg and Waters, 1985). Both noted that such things happen but did not attempt to explore further how that could be so. Yet, if strategy is attributable to an observable 'pattern' in a stream of decisions taken rather than from a pre-formulated strategic plan, then from where does the pattern come? What other regulatory forces can account for the *patterned consistency* of decisions taken that might retrospectively account for this 'emergent strategy'? This crucial question remains unanswered by advocates of the emergent strategy school.

It is here that recourse to the 'practice turn' in social theory (Bourdieu, 1990; Dreyfus, 1991; Schatzki et al., 2001; Chia, 2004; MacKay et al., 2021) can help explain the unplanned consistency of collective actions and decisions taken in any social context. According to important insights from this practice turn, sociocultural practices contain a *habitus* or modus operandi (Bourdieu, 1990) that can ensure a non-deliberate patterned consistency of responses on the part of members of a social collective even if there are no explicit plans, rules or instructions. This modus operandi, applied within an organisational context, is what makes emergent strategy possible.

Purposive Action and Modus Operandi as the Source of 'Patterned' Responsiveness

The 'practice turn' in social theory provides us with a new vocabulary and set of concepts to help understand how a patterned consistency in collective actions can emerge non-deliberately and *purposively* rather than deliberately and *purposefully*. This distinction between purposive and purposeful action is crucial for appreciating the significance of the practice turn. For Dreyfus (1991: 93, emphasis original), action 'can be *purposive* without the actor having in mind a *purpose*'. Purposive action describes a spontaneous and non-deliberate coping response elicited by the solicitations and demands of a situation. There is an immediate unthought urgency about such purposive coping responses. Purposeful action, on the other hand is more deliberate, rational and calculative; it 'presupposes having a desired and clearly articulated end goal that we aspire towards' (Chia and Holt, 2009: 92). Purposeful action assumes that thought must always precede action and is thus associated with the ubiquitous strategic planning approach. While purposeful action is goal-driven, purposive action *is about searching and discovering our goals* as we go along through our spontaneous coping responses (March, 1972: 420); it is prospective 'wayfinding' action reaching out into the as-yet-unknown (Ingold, 2000; Chia and Holt, 2009). It assumes that we can only 'know as we go' (Ingold, 2000: 228) and not beforehand.

The 'pattern' in a stream of decisions that Mintzberg and others observe in their 'emergent' strategy approach is better explained through recourse to purposive rather than purposeful action. It is action driven by the socially transmitted mechanism of *habitus* or modus operandi (Bourdieu, 1990). Modus operandi (henceforth the term we will use here) describes an organisation's tacitly shared, historically shaped pattern of social practices. It is what ensures the non-deliberate patterned consistency of responses taken by members of an organisation in a wide variety of circumstances. For any social collective such as an organisation, therefore, modus operandi is a matter-of-fact, accepted way of doing things and responding to situations internalised by its members. It is a collectively shared predisposition that expresses itself in a multitude of ways including a preferred way of organising organisational relationships, of addressing operational situations, of dealing with environmental challenges, of dealing with regulatory bodies and of arranging productive activities within the whole organisation. Modus operandi is inherently 'strategic' because it exerts a widespread 'unthinking' predispositional influence on daily activities across all levels of the organisation. It is what ensures the patterned consistency that makes possible the inadvertent emergence of a coherent strategy.

In the absence of an explicitly formulated strategic plan, therefore, it is an organisation's shared practices containing a modus operandi that ensures patterned consistency and hence predictability in its organisational responses both internally and externally. This is the genuine insight associated with the 'practice turn' in social theory (Bourdieu, 1990). Practices contain patterned regularities and tendencies – what, how and why activities are carried out in a consistent way – that invariably influence the strategic predisposition and preferences of an organisation. The evolution and internalising of such shared practices over time and the patterned consistencies in 'strategic' responses to situations encountered, can be explained by probing practical coping actions, narratives, histories and artefacts; and by closely observing exemplary behaviours across organisational levels.

Enhancing our understanding of the strategic relevance and potential of an organisation's shared practices and its associated modus operandi enables a more complete view of strategy-making incorporating purposive as well as purposeful actions and aligning the latter with the former. Examination of practices can include any recurring, formal activities of strategy carried out by apex practitioners. But crucially, inquiring about practices also entails examining the full set of operational activities – in which the majority of organisational energy and resources are expended on a daily basis – that are typically marginalised in strategy theorising. With a unique profile, intent and potential inherent in the aggregation of its practices, an organisation's modus operandi offers a crucial reference point for understanding its innate strategic tendencies and predispositions.

This broad, systemic interpretation of strategy intimates an organisation not as a solid, substantial entity but instead as made up of a coherent 'bundle' of established sociocultural practices (Schatzki, 2005) that have material economic consequences. This is not a static view, as such bundles of shared practices are only ever 'temporarily stabilised' and always subjected to evolutionary pressures internally (e.g. learning) and externally (e.g. regulatory and environmental forces). At the core of an organisational modus operandi is a non-deliberate regularity in social and economic exchanges that allows us to describe 'what an organisation does' based on its activities. If and when the observed regularity of social and economic exchanges declines, the organisation begins to wane and dissolve as a distinct economic entity. It is practices as such that constitute an organisation and that enable it to maintain its identity and characteristics.

This combination of purposeful and purposive actions in an organisation – being effective in the present through spontaneous in situ coping whilst preparing for the future through planning – defines a *strategy which reflects and is reflected in its modus operandi*. This is SiP. Failure to recognise these two crucial sides of the same coin, and failing to ensure they are constantly aligned, can lead to material negative consequences.

ILLUSTRATIVE EXAMPLE: WHEN RIGIDLY STICKING TO A PLANNED STRATEGY GOES WRONG . . .

IBM is a multinational information technology corporation serving markets around the world. Whilst now on a sound footing, we can look back on the period of 2010–14 in IBM's existence when a fixed planned strategy ended up out of step with the views of many stakeholders, and with contextual challenges and environmental trends with disastrous consequences.

A formal five-year strategy – known as 'Roadmap 2015' – was set by Sam Palmisano, then CEO, in 2010 and inherited by his successor, Ginni Rometty, in 2012. Roadmap 2015 was an expression of how Palmisano's central promise to investors at IBM of achieving $20 earnings per share (EPS) by 2015 would be realised. Palmisano had previously presided over a doubling of earnings per share in 'Roadmap 2010'.

Whilst the goals and plans of Roadmap 2015 were initially lauded by investors, to many employees and industry commentators the dedication to 'Roadmap 2015' did severe damage to the long-term prospects for IBM. According to Forbes, an unrelenting focus on delivering the main $20 EPS goal of Roadmap 2015, resulted in relentless cost-cutting; loss of experienced staff; atrophying of technical expertise; increased control bureaucracy; a lack of agility; stifling of innovation; top-down coercion; sagging staff morale and an unclear strategic future (Denning, 2014).

When Rometty took over as CEO in 2012, she initially opted to stick with Roadmap 2015 before abandoning it a year early as profits collapsed and revenue continued to fall despite EPS remaining on schedule. The realised consequences of Roadmap 2015 were threatening the sustainability of the organisation and requiring ever more elaborate financial engineering, debt and non-standard accounting practices to stick to the EPS goals.

On the news of Roadmap 2015 being abandoned, an employee group at IBM issued a statement describing the 'enormous damage' and 'toxic' work environment arising from 'Roadkill 2015', arguing 'it's time IBM executives listen to their employees . . . before this once-great company is lost to executive greed and incompetence' (Fehrenbach, 2014). Analysts agreed – suggesting that flexibility, innovation and increased investment in workers were key to the long-term success of the organisation. Over subsequent years, less rigid approaches to strategy helped IBM recover to a more sustainable position, having been brought to the brink by an unswerving commitment to fulfilling a desired pre-specified strategic goal that was not aligned with the organisation's capabilities and modus operandi.

Strategy-in-Practices (SiP)

Emphasising the immanence of SiP in an organisation's modus operandi doesn't mean disregarding what we already know of strategy or abandoning formal organisational strategising activities. Rather, it adds to our understanding of how truly effective strategy-making that produces measurable desired outcomes happens in practice through alignment of the tacit with the explicit. SiP enables us to understand how strategic propensity is always already contained in the modus operandi of an organisation and how that is shaped by the sociocultural history of the organisation operating within the context of the totality of internal and external forces exerting evolutionary pressure on its everyday activities.

In this Element we explore and elaborate on SiP in order to provide a conceptual gateway for readers to better appreciate how inadvertent strategy emergence is possible and how that inevitably underpins any more formalised attempt to develop a coherent strategy that is suited to individual organisational circumstances. As a much-overlooked but ever-present aspect of organisational strategy-making, SiP provides the missing pieces to the puzzle of 'how can we improve or sustain the effectiveness of strategy in our organisation?' This Element is intended to prompt re-evaluation of how practitioners and researchers construe the practice of strategy-making within the context of broader sociocultural forces and accrued operational expertise.

The value of a SiP perspective is that the strategic tendencies encoded in an organisation's modus operandi, whilst pervasive and powerful, tend to be tacit and unarticulated and so not widely acknowledged as an important influencing force in strategy-making. Refining our understanding of the relationship between an organisation's modus operandi and its formalised strategy can highlight new areas for improvement and value creation in strategy-making through better strategic realignment.

We have already highlighted the common treatment of strategy as a calculated, top-down process in which apex practitioners formulate plans for purposeful action. By weaving into the understanding of strategy-making an appreciation of the internally cultivated sensitivities, capabilities and predispositions of an organisation that is contained in its modus operandi, we are better able to tap into a distinctive resource that helps unlock performance potential for that organisation in the short and long run. We will explore more why and how this can be the case in the sections that follow.

The central point we make here is that in studying organisational strategy-making, it is crucial to be aware of how inherited sociocultural practices and locally honed operational capabilities congeal into a shared organisational modus operandi that then orient its members towards certain priorities, decisions and preferred courses of action. To illustrate this much-overlooked strategic reality, MacKay et al. (2021), following Jarrett and Huy (2018), used the example of how sociocultural practices in the rural province of Smaland materially shaped the emergent strategy of the Swedish furniture chain IKEA. Since origination, IKEA's modus operandi has been 'infused with the sociocultural sensibilities of Smaland (the region where IKEA originated from) and its egalitarian, hard-working and resourceful peasant culture' (MacKay et al., 2021: 1358), in which local in situ practical solutions to enduring operational challenges are emphasised. This attitude is manifested in the now signature 'flatpack' format for IKEA's products, the idea for which arose from a practical-coping concern; how to fit a leaf-shaped table into the boot of a car. The simple practical solution was to take the legs off! Thus, came the idea of 'flat-packing' its products. When applied at scale, this product format delivered effective cost performance outcomes and competitive advantage for IKEA. From local coping actions taken to resolve and overcome immediate problems and difficulties faced, IKEA thus ended up adopting a functionalist, geometric and minimalist approach to design that found resonance in markets further afield (Brownlee, 2016).

ILLUSTRATIVE EXAMPLE: HOW SOCIOCULTURAL PRACTICES INFLUENCED THE eBAY VERSUS ALIBABA OUTCOME

MacKay et al.'s (2021) comparative study of eBay's and Alibaba's strategic entry into the Chinese e-commerce market revealed substantial differences in the approaches adopted by the two organisations. The former chose acquisition of a local company as the fastest, preferred mode of entry, introducing an American-style auction and fee-charging approach that did not go down well with the engrained sociocultural preferences of Chinese customers.

Alibaba, on the other hand grew their platform by providing 'freemium' access for local manufacturers/retailers without charging anything for their product displays. Ignoring the auction method, street-style 'haggling' was instead encouraged on the Alibaba platform to simulate actual sociocultural practices favoured by Chinese customers.

In haggling, prices start from a high and eventually gravitate to an agreed lower level so that both parties, seller and buyer, feel happy that they have made a good deal. In auctioning, through blind bidding prices start low and move upwards until the successful transaction goes to the highest bidder. The 'blindness' is unsettling because you never know if your bid is good enough or if you had overbid. The rejection of the auctioning mechanism and its fee-charging approach by the Chinese public led to eBay exiting the Chinese market in December 2006.

The difference in strategic approaches by both eBay and Alibaba, proved crucial in terms of eventual outcomes in the context of the pervasive influence of local sociocultural practices favouring haggling

(MacKay et al., 2021: 1356–9).

Broader sociocultural influences inevitably permeate strategic predispositions and preferences and hence choices in an organisation. However, over time, and through its own set of unique historical experiences operating in a specific context, each organisation develops its own idiosyncratic 'variant' of its acquired sociocultural practices over time. Through honed sensitivity to local circumstances, creative and practical coping responses guided by prevalent practices are forged by organisational members to meet the specific needs of the situations faced. Each environmental encounter offers the potential to observe, learn, revise and adjust accrued practices to ensure greater effectiveness. As practitioners notice the difference between expected and realised outcomes, and experiment with nuanced alterations to better attain outcomes of interest, so practical learning occurs. This tacit form of learning fuels refinement of practitioner sensitivity to the affordances (the full set of situational possibilities) proffered by the extant environment as well as the efficacy of specific practices available.

The individual and collective learning arising from these myriad encounters are remembered and inscribed into the unique history of an organisation, influencing – often even in very minor ways – the organisational modus operandi that eventually shapes strategic tendencies. As 'variant' practices accumulate, so emerges a unique and even idiosyncratic modus operandi that sets an organisation apart from its competitors. The aggregate effect of practitioners' encounters with their operating environment and the multitude of local coping actions taken contributes to the fashioning of this organisational modus operandi. Clearly, some established practices within an organisation will be indistinguishable from competitors because of shared industry recipes (Spender, 1989). For example, practices in complying with adoption of regulatory safety standards may be deliberately shared between competing organisations for mutual benefit. Yet others are idiosyncratic to the organisation because of its unique accumulated history of encounters. Organisational modus operandi can thus be thought of as being constituted by a specific combination of such common and distinctive practices, unique to that organisation's historical pathway.

Modus operandi describes a socially embedded, unique strategic resource with potential for unique value creation that is an ever-present influence on the practical coping and creative responses of organisational members. Consequently, those responsible for running an organisation would be wise to recognise the existence of the modus operandi and astutely tap its potential for strategic advantage. It also stands to reason that failing to consider the modus operandi in formal strategy work risks setting deliberately formulated plans in direct opposition to potentially powerful sources of inertia and even possible resistance within the organisation. Aside from possibly thwarting the accomplishment of desired performance outcomes, modus operandi can generate resistances that actually act as a suffocating, passive source of obstruction to organisational aspirations. To be effective, therefore, strategic plans must contain the imprints of the organisation's accrued predispositions, capabilities and expertise as manifested in its modus operandi; these shared tendencies and predispositions must be factored in for success in strategy-making.

In operating conditions characterised by relentless change and high uncertainty, incorporating this nuanced understanding of modus operandi into formal strategy-making increases the potential for coping or even thriving through 'on the hoof' responses to unexpected and unforeseen challenges. Harnessing habituated capabilities to respond effectively to uncertain circumstances constitutes what has been called organisational resilience (i.e. elasticity under pressure). In the absence of stability in operating conditions, strategising that mobilises such resilience is what can pull an organisation through uncertain times.

Organisational leaders typically resort to predictive methods such as scenario analysis to expand thinking about new possibilities and to loosen attachment to fixed views of the world (Burt et al., 2017). Such methods can only build preparedness for a limited range of plausible developments and are vulnerable to the limitations of underpinning assumptions. In disrupted environments that confound our modelling assumptions we are often without sufficient time to rethink such analytical efforts. The significant challenges to how we work, live and trade thrown up by the current Covid pandemic, for example, provides ample evidence for how such predictive strategy methods fail in the face of an unexpected evolving reality.

One might then ask: 'How else can we deal with a future that is inherently uncertain and ambiguous, unknown and even unknowable?' Formal strategy activities may remain useful sites of analyses, conversations, interactions and decisions for understanding dynamic environmental challenges and their possible consequences. But greater attention needs to be paid to the nuanced understandings that underpin true human resilience. Such innate creative coping capabilities and adaptability inherent in an organisation's modus operandi are what help guide appropriate strategic responses. In unprecedented and highly turbulent environmental circumstances, it is these finely honed, in situ coping capabilities that will see an organisation through.

Mêtis as the Source of Ongoing Organisational Practical Coping and Strategising Efforts

All living systems contain within themselves an impulse for survival and growth. It is what impels them to relentlessly search for appropriate footholds to bootstrap to ever-higher levels of existence and greater degrees of freedom from environmental constraints (Sahlins and Service, 1960). This same built-in *élan vital* (Bergson, 1911/1998) or 'life force' pervades organisations and their members expressing itself in the form of a survivalist capability well exemplified in the Ancient Greek concept of '*mêtis*' or 'cunning intelligence' (see Detienne and Vernant's (1978) classic treatise on this ancient form of knowing). *Mêtis* describes the deep expertise and practical intelligence accrued through extended close-quarter engagement with an extant environment. *Mêtis* draws on locally honed perceptual sensitivity to environmental solicitations to intervene effectively in response to unfolding and changeable environmental conditions.

To take an example, Scott (1998) notes that in seamanship the difference between navigation and piloting illustrates how *mêtis* differs qualitatively from the more established form of knowledge that Aristotle (1998) calls *episteme*. When a cargo ship approaches a port:

> the captain typically turns the control of his vessel over to a local pilot, who brings it in to the harbour and to its berth . . . This sensible procedure designed to avoid accidents, reflects the fact that navigation on the open sea (a more abstract space) is the more general skill, while piloting a ship through traffic in a particular port is a highly contextual skill . . . What the pilot knows are local tides and currents along the coast and estuaries, the unique features of local wind and wave patterns, shifting sand bars, unmarked reefs, seasonal changes in microcurrents, local traffic conditions (Scott, 1998: 316–17).

Navigation and piloting require quite distinctly different skills and capabilities. Were the pilot to take all duties including open sea navigation, their local expertise would diminish through reduced exposure and practice. What results from this organisational practice of using skilled local expertise (*mêtis*) in combination with alternative open sea knowledge (*episteme*) is an optimised set of outcomes for all involved.

Mackay et al. (2014: 423) propose that *mêtis* can be thought of as the 'situated resourcefulness' of practitioners directly involved in everyday strategising.

Nurtured by shared practices and a sharpened observational sensitivity to environmental affordances honed through lived experiences, *mêtis* enables effective local practical coping, especially in fluid and dynamically challenging circumstances. Beyond intuition, *mêtis* is knowing when and how to skilfully manoeuvre and make the best of the affordances that circumstances throw up, achieving maximal outcomes with a minimal use of effort and resources. Such wily intelligence underpins the capacity for coping with the most unexpected of circumstances far beyond any insights or understanding arising from logical analysis or strategic plans.

Scott (1998) charts the integral role of *mêtis* in the advancement of civilisation, noting that no grand scheme of humankind has ever succeeded but for the creativity and resourcefulness of those charged with delivering it. Through actions grounded in *mêtis*, skilful and effective refinements to shared practices accrue over time that are particularly suited for coping with vague, uncertain and difficult situations. There is significant, hard-to-replicate strategic value in mêtic knowing that cannot be expressed through reason, logic or linguistic representation (Polanyi, 1966). However, as a form of knowing that resists quick accumulation and that may be more present outside than inside top management teams, *mêtis* has been marginalised or overlooked as a consideration in contemporary strategy-making approaches. By tapping *mêtis* wherever it resides within an organisation alongside formalised strategising activity, it is possible to create more productive routes for engaging with an extant environment to improve organisational effectiveness in defensive or opportunity-seeking manoeuvres. This is the real potential of modus operandi as SiP.

Illustrative Example: Mêtis as a Strategy of the Weak

Detienne and Vernant (1978) retell the story of a chariot race in ancient Greece featured in Homer's *Iliad*. The tale describes how a young charioteer, Antilocus, is able to claim a race prize despite having poor equipment and slower horses. Seemingly bound to lose before the race starts, Antilocus draws on the cunning intelligence of *mêtis* to compensate for a lack of ample resources. Before the race, surveying the course and receiving advice from his father, Antilocus observed an opportunity to swiftly turn around a stump with two white stones located at a 'narrowing of the road' caused by heavy rainfall the night before; a skill at which he is particularly good. While a less skilled driver would let his horses take a wider berth at the turn, Antilocus is able to hold his horses tight to the post. In the actual race, Antilocus skilfully executes this move at exactly the right moment, surprising a number of rivals that he is then able to outstrip in the last stretch. It is 'through *mêtis* that the charioteer triumphs over his rivals ... the man who knows the tricks wins the day even with mediocre horses' (Homer's Iliad, in Detianne and Vernant, 1978: 12). *Mêtis* is a situational skill that conjures means to overcome the odds in tricky situations and that makes the most of contextual possibilities. *Mêtis* is often a strategy of the weak or of those not in positions of power. It allows them to cope effectively even in disadvantaged and disadvantageous situations.

Being able to manufacture advantages out of oftentimes seemingly disadvantageous situations, even for a fleeting moment to gain a foothold, is fundamental to how the human species has been able to lift itself to ever-higher levels of existence: surviving, thriving and extending its degrees of freedom from environmental constraints via its cultivated mêtic capabilities. Such progress typically entails a 'passage from less to greater energy exploitation, lower to higher levels of integration, and lesser to greater all-round adaptability' (Sahlins and Service, 1960: 22). Through the ages, higher productivity, better organisation and increased adaptability to environmental circumstances have often been realised through mêtic capabilities transmitted through sociocultural practices and tacitly shared in communities.

This same reliance on mêtic capabilities applies equally to an organisational context and especially to effective strategy-making. Mainly through practical demonstration and exemplars rather than spoken means we inherit tacit 'know-how' about what it means to be part of a specific organisation, how to orient ourselves to its ways and how to act appropriately within its context. Incorporating wisdom and learning from observation of past events, socioculturally transmitted practices collectively constitute a modus operandi that prepares us to meet the varying demands we face on a day-to-day basis. Since we often act automatically and without conscious association with explicit intentions, we frequently don't acknowledge the strategic role that such shared practices play in enabling us to operate effectively. Yet, it is precisely in circumstances of rapid change and uncertainty that internalised practices, coupled with a finely honed sensitivity to local circumstances, guide our spontaneous purposive responses with a speed and efficacy that formal strategic planning approaches cannot match.

With keener observation it can be shown that such pragmatic organisational responses to disruptive change are infused with *mêtis* and inevitably reflect tacit know-how and capabilities inherent in the organisation's modus operandi. In this regard, in contrast to mainstream models of formal strategy-making, local situational sensitivity and expertise is privileged over general analysis in strategising when facing unstable and rapidly changing environments. Exhibiting this approach may be referred to as strategic agility – an 'antifragile' capacity (Taleb, 2013) that enables effective coping with, and even benefiting from, disruptions, shocks and surprises arising in the operating environment. In these uncertain situations, strategic efforts are directed towards creating an enabling environment for accrued practices and mêtic expertise inherent in the modus operandi to be deployed to maximum advantage. Going against top-down initiatives, it may mean having to abandon conventional role expectations and hierarchical habits and liberating capable practitioner expertise to meet the demands of the situation as exemplified in the following FinServe example.

CASE EXAMPLE: SHORTCUTTING FORMAL PROCESSES FOR STRATEGIC AGILITY UNDER PRESSURE

Through one of the author's associations with FinServe (a pseudonym for a FTSE100-listed financial services firm), an episode of strategic resilience and agility was encountered during the fallout of the financial crisis of 2007–8. Like most financial services organisations at the time, previously routine ways of doing business for FinServe were being disrupted by rapidly changing customer behaviours, panicking regulatory bodies and shifts in the global financial competitive landscape. Politicians had started to intervene in an unprecedented way in the activities of the sector. It was against this backdrop that the CEO of FinServe was contacted by a senior member of the UK government. The conversation was short and to the point – with government backing, would FinServe acquire BusSoc, a competitor that was in financial distress? The senior government figure required an answer within twenty-four hours.

The immediate reaction from the CEO was that it was an excellent opportunity to acquire competitor assets at a favourable price whilst generating significant political capital at the heart of government. The CEO also estimated that during stable times, the due diligence (acquisition decision) process for such a proposition would have taken nine months. Recognising the exceptional nature of this request, the CEO summoned all employees – regardless of level – that would normally have been involved in due diligence processes into the largest meeting room in the organisation. Confidentiality agreements were signed, sustenance was supplied and the assembled experts were tasked with advising the CEO within twenty-four hours of what his answer to the government should be.

Without a precedent of formal processes to follow, an improvised marketplace of ideas sprung up. Those involved in this 'due diligence lock-in' described a mixture of feelings including exhilaration, inclusion, respect, accountability and unparalleled creative licence as they were asked to rise to the challenge. In a dynamic and intense blend of short-lived conversations, interactions, analyses and workshopping of ideas, the *mêtis* of expert colleagues from across the organisation was tapped in a collaborative show of collective decision-making. Within twenty-four hours, the CEO was advised that the collective view was that the acquisition should be declined, on account of a number of risks and incompatibilities discovered. The CEO accepted and communicated this outcome to the FinServe board and the UK government. BusSoc was eventually acquired by UKFin, one of FinServ's competitors.

FinServe tracked with interest the outcomes of BusSoc's acquisition, which proved damaging to UKFin's performance over the following years, even with government support. The insights developed in the creative chaos of the twenty-four-hour 'due diligence lock-in' emerged to be as, if not more, accurate than the analytical outcomes of previous nine-month acquisition decision processes. Despite this experience, as the intense disruption of the financial crisis receded, FinServe reverted to their formal due diligence processes for subsequent acquisition appraisals.

Recognising the existence of SiP can help an organisation fashion competitive advantages out of chaotic situations that confound others. This capacity for 'strategic agility' arises from the shared practices forged and refined by the historical experiences of those in the organisation (Nayak et al., 2019). In this way, strategic agility can be said to be 'path dependent' – drawing on learning from prior immersion in productive activities and experiences. What may start as a gradual adjustment to the slightest of environmental changes detected by an individual can snowball via feedback loops, social exchange and a variety of learning modes into the creative forging of shared, effective practices. Accumulated practical know-how enables organisational members to effectively fashion, time and again, appropriate responses to novel environmental challenges. Tangible moments of organisational advantage may arise when the design of formal processes allows those with practical insights to become involved in strategising. This is how the potential of SiP can be accessed; by inviting into formal strategy activities those with lived experience of small advantage-gaining actions and mêtic capabilities.

To harness the power of SiP means infusing organisational strategising with an appreciation of the influence of inherited sociocultural perceptions, practices and predispositions on strategic choices. It is unlikely that this know-how will reside exclusively within a top management team. Thus, drawing on SiP requires an opening up of formal strategy processes to a broader range of organisational practitioners at all levels (Whittington, 2019). If the aim is to maximise organisational performance potential, from a SiP perspective strategy-making must reach beyond the board room to the multitude of operational, learning and coping actions happening daily across organisational levels. To commit to working with SiP means seeking ways to conduct strategy-making within broader socialisation processes and cultural expectations for optimal outcomes. This includes exploring how to harness 'natural' organisational responses to emergent situations and environmental affordances that have been shaped by sociocultural imperatives.

Working with SiP necessitates inclusive formal strategy processes that acknowledge and build on contributions made by organisational members and groups across levels of the organisation. Understood thus, strategy-making becomes not just a prerogative of top management (although apex practitioners remain important actors). Instead, strategy-making permeates the entire organisation as an ongoing process – involving to varying extents – the practical nous, capabilities and talents of all its members. Rather than conceiving of strategy as some *thing* that happens at the top of an organisation, strategy is instead re-imagined as a continuing *process* running throughout the organisations' dynamic system of productive activity. This fundamental reframing of strategy-making, whilst arguably carrying multiple benefits, challenges established hierarchical arrangements and power bases in most set-ups. To reframe strategy-making requires energy, effort and an open mentality from those in formal positions of power, and may carry feelings of risk and questionable payback.

To make a stronger case for why a SiP approach to strategy-making is worth pursuing, we will examine the limitations of the dominant substantialist worldview underpinning the top-down strategic planning approach and how that affects our understanding of the role of human action in creating social and economic advantage. We will then articulate an alternative processual worldview which embraces uncertainty, volatility and changefulness as primary conditions of reality, and explore the implications for strategy practitioners and strategy-making practices of embracing processual insights. From this alternative processual world view, the value of local coping actions, practices and mêtic know-how is shown to be critical to effective strategising.

2 A Processual Worldview: Implications for Language, Thought and Action in Strategy-Making

(T)he actual world is a process, and that ... process is the becoming of actual entities.

Whitehead (1929/1978: 30)

Continuity of change, preservation of the past in the present, real duration ... life, like conscious activity, is invention, is unceasing creation.

Bergson (1911/1998: 23)

In this section, we:

- Examine the influence of a *substantialist* worldview on our perceptions of reality and its associated implications for strategy and strategy-making.
- Elaborate on the consequences of adopting an alternative *processual* worldview for the framings of the world of human affairs and hence its implications for strategy-making.
- Critically re-examine the relationship between language, thought and knowledge in relation to effective action.
- Point to the dangers of mistaking abstract representations for reality itself
- Show how a *processual* worldview leads to emphasising the importance of unmediated action.
- Show how prospective, *purposive* action forms an integral part of effective strategising.

As social creatures, we inherit a collectively shared worldview that predisposes us to act, think and make sense of, in culturally specific ways. This inherited worldview contains assumptions and commonly held beliefs about the nature of reality and how to best engage and deal with it effectively. In general, any worldview is made up of an 'observational order' that directs us to attend to selective aspects of our lived experiences of the world, and a 'conceptual order' comprising a 'rough system of ideas' in terms of which we subsequently interpret our experiences (Whitehead, 1933: 183). Our understanding of the world, as such, is not simply 'dictated by impartial facts'. Rather, what is selected and retained 'is rearranged in a subjective order of prominence' (Whitehead, 1933: 183). 'Facts' do not simply 'speak for themselves'. Instead, we actively impute significance to selective aspects of our lived experiences and so to 'fabricate' facts (Latin, *factum*, *facere*- to make) out of them.

Novel observations may help modify our conceptual order and likewise, novel concepts point to new ways of understanding our lived experiences. Thus, our worldview may evolve over time as we interact with others, pass through educational systems, accrue life experiences, and reflect on their implications for guiding thoughts, actions and decisions. Whilst always present in the background, this ever-refining worldview is not usually the focus of our attention and so we are mostly unaware of how it shapes and influences our preferences, thoughts and actions. Nevertheless, it provides a socially structured context for shaping how we understand and engage with the world.

In the introductory section, we noted that the top-down strategic planning approach is tied to a still-dominant substantialist worldview, a legacy of thought passed down from the Greek philosopher Parmenides in the fifth century BC. This substantialist – as in 'substance' – worldview assumes that ultimate reality comprises discrete, stable and substantial entities. As such, fragments of reality can be isolated, identified, described, known and shared through linguistic and other symbolic representations (e.g. mathematics). Because of this assumption of discreteness and isolatability, the belief is that it is possible to name, classify, order and categorise phenomena in the world using language as the primary source of knowledge.

This idea of a stable, substantialist worldview led Aristotle (1998: 4) to privilege knowing through vision as the most valuable form of knowledge (*episteme*) attainable via application of an IS/IS NOT logic of identity. Aristotelian logic makes clear how to distinguish one thing from another so that it is impossible to confuse one thing with another. Thus, 'it is impossible for anyone to suppose the same thing is and is not, as some imagine that Heraclitus says' (Aristotle, 1933: 162, our emphasis). By creating such clear-cut is/is not distinctions in language, it is possible to formulate descriptive categories for everything in the world. Should we encounter something that is hard to classify (we are not sure if it 'is' or 'is not' in a known category), the instinctive response is to refine our language and concepts, adding new (sub-)categories to our system of knowledge that will then allow us to identify unambiguously what a thing is or is not.

Aristotle called this method of knowledge-creation his 'principle of non-contradiction' and through it he was able to elevate knowledge through self-identity, stability and substance over knowledge through difference, change and process. Furthermore, change, whilst acknowledged, was considered of second-ary importance in comparison to the primacy of stable entities; yes, 'things' do change, but change is not constitutive of things! This influential Aristotelian logic and system of knowledge underpins much of contemporary economic thinking and with it the strategy literature. The dictum 'if you can't measure it, you can't manage it' is one side effect of the dominance of this substantialist worldview.

A substantialist world view values knowing through abstract symbolic representations over knowing through direct lived experience. As such, abstract categories, complex mental models and generalised principles are preferred over the primacy of the senses as the foundational basis of knowledge. Convenient boundaries are drawn around phenomena so that individual entities or classes of entities (such as industries, organisations, competitors, employees, shareholders etc.) are created to facilitate communication and cognitive manipulation. This measurement and appraisal of attributes and logical analysis is underpinned by the assumption that all other things are essentially stable and equal (*ceteris paribus*). Analytical outcomes are used as the rational basis for determining goals and associated plans to organise resource deployment and undertake initiatives – what many would identify as 'strategic planning'. Within mainstream business education, consultancy and practice, substantialist assumptions remain dominant and largely unchallenged.

In practice, however, experienced strategy practitioners know well that organisational situations are hardly ever stable and that the future is rarely a linear projection of the present. The result is that they continually struggle to anticipate with accuracy how events are likely to unfold. To cope with the inherent unknowability of the world, when conducting strategic analysis on some aspect of the future, therefore, there is a tendency to make a set of restrictive *ceteris paribus* assumptions. While there is awareness that within relevant groups (such as competitors, employees etc.) there is high variability of attributes, levels of creativity and motivation, and capacity to make a wide degree of non-rational choices (agency), to avoid being confounded by the complexity of the world, *ceteris paribus* assumptions provide a necessary, stabilising platform to allow systematic analyses and the imagination of what might become.

Yet, practical problems arise when the adoption of *ceteris paribus* assumptions becomes so habitual that they recede into the unconscious, and we end up mistaking the messy reality as experienced for the neat, simplified version presented in abstract rational analyses. In *Science and the Modern World*, the philosopher Alfred North Whitehead warned about the dangers of this tendency to mistake our abstract representations for reality itself. He called this error the 'Fallacy of Misplaced Concreteness' (Whitehead, 1926/1985: 64) and warned of the dangers of sticking rigidly to our abstractions and ignoring actual goings-on in the world. For him, any community, be it a civilisation, society or an organisation, 'which cannot burst through its current abstraction is doomed to sterility after a very limited period of progress' (Whitehead, 1926/1985: 73). We ignore our raw lived experiences at our own peril.

Because of the problems associated with the basic assumptions underpinning a substantialist worldview, attention has turned to an alternative *processual* worldview which assumes that the world is fundamentally in a permanent state of instability, flux, change and becoming. From this revised understanding, stable states are secondary abstractions from our actual, phenomenal lived experiences. It is our own intervening acts of ordering that help create a seemingly discrete, ordered and stable world that then lends itself to symbolic representation and manipulation. As such it is our selective actions of parsing out our phenomenal experiences into discrete fragments that enable thought to be possible, rather than thought guiding action. This reversal – of action preceding and facilitating thought – is vital for how we understand strategy and strategy-making from a processual perspective.

From a processual worldview, strategising does not so much happen within the realms of linguistic abstraction but instead is very much embedded in our everyday coping actions and shared practices. Instead of strategy-making taking place exclusively in boardrooms, it is happening throughout the organisation on an ongoing, and even mundane, basis. Adopting a processual worldview enables us to reconnect with an ancient tradition marginalised in modern times by the dominance of the abstract, rationalist and substantialist worldview. In the following sections, we show how SiP is better understood through this processual worldview by elevating awareness of how everyday in situ practical coping actions and shared practices provide the founding basis for organisational strategy-making.

Process Is Reality

The idea that process itself is reality has been revived and advocated by a number of twentieth-century philosophers including Alfred North Whitehead (1861–1947). Whitehead's *processual* worldview reconnects us with the claims of Heraclitus, a predecessor of Parmenides, who insisted that the world is fundamentally chaotic and perpetually fluxing and changing rather than pre-ordered, stable and substantial. Such a processual worldview is well encapsulated in the ancient Greek dictum *'panta rhei'*; everything flows and nothing abides. It presupposes a messy, chaotic and emergent context for our actions and interventions; the reality we inhabit is inherently unstable and continuously evolving and becoming rather than discrete, stable and substantial (James, 1911/1996; Bergson, 1911/1998; Bohm, 1980; Prigogine, 1989). In contrast to the substantialist worldview, a processual worldview deems that order does not pre-exist but instead emerges spontaneously through a multitude of local interactions; order emerges as temporarily stabilised patterns of coherence within a churning sea of chaos and disorder (Prigogine, 1989: 399).

As such, changes are always going on of their own accord independent of human intentions; they are 'unowned' (Rescher, 1996) rather than the result of

human interventions. Change takes place inexorably like a 'gradually expanding rubber balloon . . . assuming at each moment unexpected forms' (Bergson,
1946/1992: 96). Such unowned change is characterised by 'variations, restless
expansion, opportunistic conquests, sudden captures and offshoots' (Chia,
1999: 222; cf. Deleuze and Guattari, 1988). They do not involve a linear and
sequential 'succession of instantaneous configuration of matter' (Whitehead,
1926/1985: 63). Rather, real change is continuous and interpenetrating; the
'past . . . gnaws into the future, and . . . swells as it advances' (Bergson, 1911/
1998: 2). As such, changes take place not by 'jumps and jolts' but rather 'leak(s)
in insensibly' (James, 1909/1996: 399) much like the processes of ageing, the
breakdown of a previously loving relationship, or the slow but inexorable
erosion of riverbanks or even climate change. They are 'silent transformations'
(Jullien, 2011) occurring right under our very noses and yet we are oftentimes
unaware of them! This is a revised understanding of how global 'unowned'
change happens when understood from a processual worldview.

As previously noted, this processual worldview has its origins in ancient
times in both Western and Eastern civilisations. In the former, it is well
encapsulated in the ancient Greek philosopher Heraclitus's saying: 'You never
step into the same river twice'. For Heraclitus all objects and things are no more
than temporarily stabilised and contested manifestations of an underlying flux;
things come into being 'through opposition, and all are in flux like a river'
(Mansley-Robinson, 1968: 89). Thus, conflict, struggles, temporary advances,
reversals and precarious reconciliations are the real stuff of life. The implication
is that human will, intentions and deliberate interventions have only limited
impact in shaping eventual outcomes and destinies.

Arguably, a processual worldview resonates more with our everyday lived
experiences and in the context of strategy-making, the experiences of seasoned
practitioners who are keenly aware of the limits of their strategising capabilities.
As such, there has been a revival of interest in this processual worldview and its
consequences for theorising strategic and organisational change (e.g. Chia,
1999, 2014; Tsoukas and Chia, 2002; Weick, 2009; Hernes, 2014; Langley
and Tsoukas, 2016; Burgelman et al., 2018; Mackay et al., 2023).

This same idea that process is reality is intimated in the Eastern *Ying/Yang*
symbol and ancient Chinese texts including the *I Ching* (Book of Change) and
the philosopher Lao Tzu's *Tao Te Ching*. In the latter, there is constant allusion
to the pervasive influence of an undirected fluxing and natural force, the *Tao*,
inexorably shaping situational emergence and outcomes. *Tao* alludes to an
internal momentum and tendency of things; the latent evolutionary force containing an 'impulse . . . for change' (Chia and Holt, 2009: 30). For the ancient

Chinese, it is this formless and ever-flowing *Tao* that is the ultimate generator of the ordered world of objects, things, artefacts and their attributes.

If we embrace change as inexorable, pervasive and ever-present, we must reject the substantialist assumption that human situations are inherently stable and that we can arbitrarily impose our elaborately planned designs onto an apparently recalcitrant reality. Instead, from a processual worldview, dealing with change requires us to begin with our senses by sensitively 'reading' the internal propensity of situations faced and then using this understanding to creatively channel the energy and momentum contained therein towards our desired outcomes. Here, timing and timeliness of insertion, not size, scale or force of intervention, are crucial. A heightened sensitivity and nuanced appreciation of the unfolding complexity of circumstances is what enables us to make effective strategic responses rather than rigidly adhering to any pre-established strategic plans. Such in situ responsiveness depends more on the senses than the intellect (Dreyfus, 1991; Chia and Holt, 2009). To fully appreciate the significance of adopting this processual worldview for our understanding of strategy-making, however, we first need to examine the relationship between language and thought, and the limits of representational knowledge.

Language, Thought and Representational Knowledge

Language is often thought of as merely a medium for communicating thought. In fact, language plays a fundamentally constitutive role in shaping our perception and thought in a way that is not well appreciated. The structural linguist Ferdinand de Saussure (1966: 111) points out that 'our thought – apart from its expression in words – is only a shapeless and indistinct mass'. Likewise, for philosopher Martin Heidegger (1971: 134), 'it is in words and language that things first come into Being and are'. Our language constitutes our world rather than represents it.

Language, and in particular the alphabetic system of writing, has immeasurably shaped Western perceptions, predispositions and paradigms of thought and hence their associated societal preoccupations, priorities and practices (McLuhan, 1962; Ong, 1967; Havelock, 1982). McLuhan and Logan (1977: 373–4) maintain that the invention of the alphabet inspired several intellectual innovations that form the foundational basis of Western thought including especially 'abstract science, formal logic, and individualism'. McLuhan and McLuhan (1988: 15–17) insist that: 'Prolonged mimesis of the alphabet and its fragmenting properties' led to the Greeks privileging the substantialist idea of 'atomicity' – the idea that all of matter comprise tiny discrete atoms. They drew an analogy with 'what the alphabet had done to language and likened their atoms to letters … ' (Havelock, 1976: 51). As such, the substantialist world-view, with its emphasis on discrete, atomistic, stable and substantial entities, is a direct result of the alphabetisation of the Western mind.

As previously pointed out, the substantialist worldview inspired the development of Aristotelian logic (Ong, 1967, 1982) and the form of representational knowledge, *episteme* (a communicable, scientific form of knowledge) associated with it. This is the dominant form of knowledge produced in academic research and it underpins the top-down strategic planning approach championed in the strategy literature. It rests on the unchallenged belief that reality can be conceptually represented accurately through language and then systematically acted upon; effective action is predicated upon prior conceptual comprehension so that thought always precedes action.

From a processual worldview, however, language – whilst offering useful approximations for convenient mental manipulation – is inherently incapable of accurately representing an ever-changing, fluxing totality. Language is useful for parsing, fixing and naming selective aspects of our sensual datum and for creating concepts and categories to aid abstract analyses and to impute causal relations, but they are essentially abstractions. Thus, 'in the sky "constellations", on the earth "beach", "sea", "cliff", "bushes" … Out of time we cut "days" and "nights", "summers" and "winters". We say *what* each part of the sensible continuum is and all these abstract *whats* are concepts' (James, 1911/1996: 50, emphasis original). The result is we habitually think in such fixed categories without realising they are relatively arbitrary distinctions.

The act of 'languaging' the world is a shared social practice that enables us to collectively forge a stable 'surrogate' social reality to which we are then able to respond meaningfully and productively. However, as approximations, the categories making up this social reality are not without problems. For example, when exactly does day become night? Or summer become winter? There is a certain arbitrariness about these distinctions that ultimately depends on social consensus. Categories may serve a useful practical function, but they are not able to accurately capture a moving and unfolding reality.

The philosopher Henri Bergson (1911/1998: 306) points out that because of this representational limitation, we inevitably resort to a 'cinematographic method'; taking numerous 'snapshots' of passing reality and then attempting to join them back together to create a rough *approximation* of the flow of our lived experiences. The result, however, is paradoxically the creation of an unbridgeable gap between the '*cinematographic character of our knowledge of things*' and the 'infinite multiplicity of changes and becomings that passes before our eyes' (Bergson, 1911/1998: 304, emphasis original) in actuality. What we experience and what we are able to communicate through language are not the same. Linguistic terms do not reflect reality and we mistake one for the other at our own peril! This is what Whitehead (1926/1985) meant by the 'Fallacy of Misplaced Concreteness'.

Language and symbolic systems (including mathematics) may be useful and convenient 'tools' for parsing, fixing and naming selective aspects of our lived experiences for functional purposes. Language allows us to interact with others in creating arbitrary social orders (albeit not without some missteps along the way) that make life more liveable for all. And language helps make situations 'work' for us in pragmatically useful terms, but in so doing it also distorts our understanding of reality. What 'works' must be distinguished from what is 'true'.

ILLUSTRATIVE EXAMPLE: 'THIS IS NOT A PIPE . . . '

In 1929, the Belgian surrealist painter René Magritte produced a painting entitled *The Treachery of Images* now on display at the Los Angeles County Museum of Art. The painting depicts a pipe and is accompanied by a placard stating: '*Ceci n'est pas une pipe*', meaning '*This is not a pipe*'. Magritte describes the public response to his painting thus:

'How people reproached me for it! And yet, could you stuff my pipe? No, it's just a representation, is it not? So, if I had written on my picture "This is a pipe," I'd have been lying!' (Magritte, in Torczyner, 1977: 71).

In insisting on the validity of stating 'This is not a pipe' Magritte was directing our attention to the common tendency to mistake our representations for reality; for mistaking the map for the territory, the menu for the dish, for our overreliance on statistics, graphs, reports etc. and hence for the tendency to over rely on pre-formulated strategic plans to guide our actions.

The Limits of Representational Knowledge and the Importance of Unmediated Action

Abstract representational knowledge is useful in facilitating social and economic exchanges, but as an approximation of reality it invariably 'falsifies as well as omits' (James, 1911/1996: 79). Systems of language and symbolic representation enable us to construct a social reality that helps us deal collectively with the uncertainties and ambiguities of life. The modicum of order and predictability provided by language-based representations allows us to render more *liveable* a world constantly in flux. But while language, concepts and theories serve a useful practical function, a processual worldview reminds us that they DO NOT represent reality as it is.

This is why our abstract theories often seem to lag lived experience. Theories are products of retrospective reasoning, but life is lived prospectively – a point the Danish philosopher Soren Kierkegaard (Kierkegaard, 1843) was at pains to make in his reflections. Logic and reason are used post-facto to explain what has happened after it has happened. Living, on the other hand, is the prospective act of reaching out into the as-yet-unknown. Oftentimes the act precedes the comprehension.

From a processual worldview, therefore, raw sensing and pure unmediated action often precede thought and cognitive representation; the reality is we often *act before we think*! Such pure 'prospective' actions serve as 'dynamos for change' by rendering explicit what was tacit and hence revealing the potential 'latent in (ourselves) and (our) world' (Cooper, 1976: 1002). Consequently, when faced with the unknown, we are impelled to initiate prospective, purposive actions to remove the unsettling ambiguity and equivocality with which we are confronted. Uncertainty is thus what prompts a prospective, purposive response, for were we certain things would come aright by themselves, there would be no need to act (von Mises, 1949/1998: 105); action presupposes uncertainty.

A processual worldview leads to the realisation that our pure, unmediated actions help *discover* and *reveal* rather than *realise* our goals (March, 1972: 420). Such *active responsiveness* begins with the senses; perceiving, noticing, differentiating and attending to ongoing perturbations, solicitations and environmental affordances. This primary sensing activity serves as a pre-cognitive basis for the subsequent development of capabilities, skilled performances and eventual mastery (Polanyi, 1966; Dreyfus, 2002; Nayak et al., 2019). That such unmediated sensing and detection of fine differences could form the basis for the cultivation of organisational capabilities is largely absent from strategy theorising. But curiously, it is explicitly advocated in business practices in some non-Western cultures (Matsushita, 2002; Inamori, 2014).

The limitations of a substantialist worldview with its emphasis on abstract representational knowledge (e.g. concepts, theories, reports, plans etc.) have not been sufficiently countenanced in mainstream strategy theorising. The intellectual distortions associated with abstract representations help explain why elaborate strategic plans often go awry. These shortcomings are a result of the essential partiality and selectivity of language and logic in capturing some aspects of a moving reality whilst ignoring others. 'Facts' are not as self-evident as they might appear.

The trade-off for overly relying on abstract representational knowledge is a selective blindness that can eventually come back to haunt us in the form of unintended consequences (Merton, 1936). Focusing attention on that which is of immediate interest to us concurrently marginalises other important aspects of reality and their possible future consequences. Merton (1936: 901) refers to this tendency as the 'imperious immediacy of interest'; a tendency to be overly preoccupied with our immediate concerns so that it leads us to exclude a careful consideration of the future unintended consequences of an action currently taken. Eschewing representational knowledge means getting back to the 'rough ground' where things actually happen on an everyday basis (Dunne, 1997).

ILLUSTRATIVE EXAMPLE: MANAGEMENT BY WALKING AROUND

Procter and Gamble (P&G) is a multinational consumer goods firm reaching customers in over 180 countries. Since being established in Cincinnati, Ohio in 1837, P&G has steadily grown its portfolio of brands and operations to reach a $71bn turnover organisation employing over 100,000 people in 2021 (www.pg.com).

Whilst the company has experienced highs and lows over its history, P&G has more often than not been praised for its business performance grounded in a commitment to staying at the forefront of innovation, branding, and manufacturing practice. Corporate communications describe an organisational aspiration to work through 'practices that improve people's lives'.

One practice famously highlighted at the heart of P&G's modus operandi in the best-selling management book *In Search of Excellence* (Peters and Waterman, 1984), is referred to as 'management by walking around'. As an ex-employee, one of the authors of this book was schooled in this practice as part of leadership training at P&G. The premise is quite simple – if you are in a managerial role, treat time spent in direct operations, whether with customers, suppliers or colleagues, as an investment with a return rather than a cost to be minimised. The information, insights and knowing arising from direct exposure to operational realities and broad social relationships will complement the vast array of abstract data and analysis at your disposal. As a consequence, you will be better able to act in an informed, effective and efficient way, dealing with issues before they escalate and sensing opportunities to be pursued at the earliest moment. The more turbulent the managerial situation faced, the more valuable these insights from first-hand experience become.

A recent conversation with an ex-colleague now running one of P&G's largest global facilities revealed that he encourages his leadership team to spend c.50 per cent of their time in direct operations. Sometimes this will be exploring or reacting to specific challenges or interests, but most often it is time spent observing, discussing and participating in routine goings-on. This is a normal, expected practice for anyone joining that leadership team. It is also an everyday part of the modus operandi of the facility, a localised version of which can be found in other manufacturing facilities for P&G around the world. As a hallmark of managerial practice in P&G, 'management by walking around' contributes to the organisation's extensive track record in running efficient, adaptable and reliable product supply operations.

Prospective Purposive Action as an Integral Feature of Effective Strategising

A presumption that deliberate intention and prior goal-setting based on representational knowledge is required for achieving successful outcomes has become, 'like the air we breathe', so 'pervading, and so seemingly necessary' (Whitehead, 1933: 21) that it is almost unthinkable to not regard this as an integral feature of any strategy-making. Yet, the belief that such abstract representations (i.e. strategic analyses, consultancy reports etc.) are needed to guide practice is often challenged by experienced practitioners facing turbulent, uncertain or shifting circumstances. They point to the perennial 'theory-practice' gap and question the relevance and usefulness of theory in guiding practice. They have a point. Underlying reasons are associated with the limits of representation as we have discussed in the previous sections. While this issue of relevance of management theory to practice has been raised by several business school academics there has been little resolution (e.g. Hitt, 1998; Pfeffer and Fong, 2002; Mintzberg, 2004; Bennis and O'Toole, 2005; Starkey and Tempest, 2009). The simple fact is that the theory–practice gap is a consequence of an unchallenged reliance on abstract representational knowledge as the primary basis for guiding decisions and action.

The result is a paradoxical situation where experienced strategy practitioners continue to spend inordinate amounts of time and effort producing elaborate strategic plans while at the same time doubting the value of such formal activities. A common, lame justification is that even if there is little value in strategic plans, the act of producing such plans helps focus the mind and assure stakeholders that executives are in control of the organisation's situation. It appears that the activity of strategic planning is frequently more about justifying and legitimising intended strategic actions than about what is actually done.

How might more effective and useful ways of strategising be achieved? If nothing else, it should begin with questioning the effectiveness of linguistic and symbolic representations in accurately capturing and representing the reality of goings-on in the world. By realising the representational limits of theories, models, maps, plans, statistics and other artefacts as aids to strategy-making, openness to complementary approaches can be encouraged (Chia, 1996; Jullien, 2000). From a processual worldview, prospective purposive actions must form an integral feature of effective organisational strategising.

3 Practices as Shared Aggregations of In Situ Practical Coping Responses

> our practices embody pervasive responses, discriminations, motor skills . . . which add up to . . . what it is to be a person, an object, an institution, etc . . . These practices do not arise from beliefs, rules, or principles.
>
> Dreyfus (1991: 17–22)

> What is shared is not a conceptual scheme . . . not a belief system that can be made explicit and justified . . . What we share is simply our average comportment.
>
> Dreyfus (1991: 155)

In this section, we:

- Show how adopting a processual worldview leads to viewing purposive action as a 'goal-seeking' activity.
- Explore how such purposive actions can inadvertently generate positive unintended outcomes for a collective.
- Show that purposive actions are guided by a repository of internalised practices containing a sociocultural modus operandi.
- Show that practices themselves are aggregations of effective coping actions that rely on the sensing and exploitation of environmental affordances.
- Show that effective practical coping begins with observational fidelity

The concepts and axioms of a processual worldview provide us with an alternative way of understanding the world of strategy-making as a purposive rather than purposeful activity. By eschewing a reliance on abstract theories and elaborate plans, strategising efforts are instead diverted to attending to immediate operating realities and the relentless search for concrete advantage-gaining opportunities in even the most dynamic and turbulent of circumstances. Extended immersion in such operating realities results in heightened sensitivity to goings-on. This sensitivity to local circumstances helps the forging of appropriate responses that further the strategising effort. Through increasing exposure to the idiosyncrasies of operating realities, involving colleagues, customers, vendors and so on, a more nuanced understanding of situational needs is cultivated; one that expands possibilities for a variety of creative responses to be initiated. Organisational members learn to develop hands-on action initiatives involving nuanced, timely adjustments that are better attuned to the flow of reality thereby nudging situations closer to desired outcomes with an economy of effort expended and with minimal negative consequences (Jullien, 1999).

ILLUSTRATIVE EXAMPLE: ACTION BEFORE STRATEGY

In 2003, Lego had diversified almost to the point of destruction. The turnaround in its fortunes over the next decade was remarkable – from a point of near-bankruptcy and dwindling sales, it evolved into the top-performing global toy company.

In an interview (Ashcroft, 2014) reflecting on the long process of strategic change, ex-CEO Jurgen V. Knudstrop observed that when the business was failing, the leaders realised the strategy was wrong, even though the underlying calculations were sound based on what had previously served the business well. To cope with the changes, the idea of a formal strategy was temporarily replaced with an action-based initiative for dealing with immediate challenges in order to build confidence and learn from the circumstances faced. Stressing its generic nature, Knudstrop emphasised the key difference in approach was diverting effort from abstract grand strategising to figuring out details and delivering outcomes with and through the 8,000 people in the organisation.

Knudstrop comments, 'The main thing I learned, and this was a major challenge for me as I'm naturally a thinker, is that you believe you need to think your way into a new way of acting, but what you actually do is *you act your way into a new way of thinking*. So, it was about less talk and more actions.' He illustrates this key pivot through an example of the introduction of an in-person, whiteboard-based reporting practice in the factories for colleagues from across levels and functions. By being together in the production environment and using low-tech manual methods and conversation to create common understanding of operating realities, 'a social mechanism that started driving change' emerged. He observed that those involved in the operational reviews didn't need to be

told how to improve performance, they simply started changing it effectively of their own volition but in a collectively coherent way. Localised
versions of this engaged practice were deployed across the business to
nurture effective coping responses to the difficult circumstances faced.

This sea change in approach to strategy – from top-down abstract
calculations to action arising from immersion in operating realities –
was integral to reversing Lego's problematic situation and beginning
a remarkable build back to profitable market leadership.

In difficult, uncertain and turbulent operating conditions, it is oftentimes
necessary to 'act your way into a new way of thinking'. This is the kind of
searching purposive action in practice that a processual worldview encourages.

Prospective Purposive Action as 'Goal-Seeking' Rather Than 'Goal-Driven'

In Section 1, we showed that purposive action can help explain the inadvertent
emergence of an unplanned yet coherent strategy. This simple re-orientation
acknowledges the presence of a tacit organisational modus operandi contained
in shared practices guiding coping actions while deeply immersed in operational realities. It points to the need for complementary alertness and sensitivity to local conditions as the foundational basis of effective strategy-making
without necessarily abandoning formal strategising activities (e.g. publication
of plans to meet shareholder expectations). It means prioritising the know-how
gleaned from extended close-quarter engagement with operational realities and
seeing the strategic potential inherent in everyday organisational practices
rather than in elaborate strategic plans. Engaging in everyday activities such
as 'strategising by walking around' increases the level, depth and intensity of
interactions, dialogue and relationship-building, and with a broader range of
stakeholders, than is allowed for by a formal top-down approach.

This kind of bottom-up strategising grounded in operating realities is not
dissimilar from the way a highly skilled carpenter expertly saws a piece of wood
along the grain to fashion what is needed with the minimal amount of material
resistance and hence with an economy of effort; purposive action often yields
maximal outcome with minimal effort. This is what defines mastery of a craft.
When renowned martial artist Bruce Lee was asked how he had attained
mastery of his craft, he responded 'the height of cultivation is really nothing
special. It is merely simplicity; the ability to express the utmost with the
minimum' (Little, 1996: 125). Lee attributed his legendary capabilities to
habituated daily practice that helped hone his skills to the point that they

enabled him to act with an economy of effort superior to that of his competitors. Thus, Lee's seemingly effortless victories belie the investment he had made in continuously honing his skill through practice away from the competitive arena to maximise his readiness for coping in subsequent encounters.

Purposive action is prospective in that it entails the seeking out of appropriate moments in the flow of events for timely interventions and to do so with a minimum of resistance involved. Compared to developing and imposing grand plans, such an approach to strategising is more nuanced, understated, less jarring, less spectacular and hence less wasteful in effort and energy expended. Effective strategic action, therefore, is not just about knowing *what* to do but also knowing *where* and *when* to act to achieve maximal gain and with minimal disruption. Thus, the most accomplished strategists are those who intervene in a timely, decisive manner with what may seem simple acts that realise disproportionately favourable outcomes. This is the ultimate consequence of embracing a processual approach to strategy-making.

Prospective, purposive actions often arise out of a felt need or a sense of disquiet. Frequently, they have a 'starting point in a dissatisfaction, and thereby a feeling of absence' (Bergson, 1911/1998: 297). Such actions can entail 'moving away from' rather than 'moving towards'; impelled by a sense of what is missing rather than by a pre-specified need. They tap on our instincts and accumulated practices in a deep, unconscious way. For example, a sense of danger causes us to retreat from the perceived threat; hunger propels us to actively search for food; unfavourable weather conditions impel us to seek shelter and so on. All this happens without much prior deliberation. They entail seeking new possibilities or moving away from unsatisfactory situations and not necessarily *towards* any pre-set end goal; they are *goal-seeking* rather than *goal-driven* actions.

Prospective *purposive* action also applies in our modern lives. Creative acts of invention, improvisation and innovation are often a response to a felt sense of dissatisfaction with the status quo. It is the 'reaching out' for as-yet undefined improvement rather than a 'homing-in' on any pre-set objective or goal. In a competitive environment, an organisation may feel impelled to improve simply to remain competitive and to avoid being left behind by its rivals, but such 'improvements' are not absolute and are only definable in relation to what its competitors are able to do. As such performative excellence cannot be pre-defined; we only know excellence *after the fact*. True excellence always surprises.

In the reality of everyday life, prospective purposive action often entails moving away from an undesirable but known situation into the unknown. For example, cutting losses through disinvestments, divorce in marriage breakdowns and forced migrations because of conflict and war; all are motivated by a need to 'get away' or escape *from* rather than move *towards* something pre-specified. This aspect of prospective purposive human action is what James March (1972: 420) was getting at when he writes about *goal-seeking* rather than *goal-driven* activity. Purposive goal-seeking activity, involving practical coping, adaptability, flexibility etc., is increasingly becoming a valuable feature of organisational strategising particularly in relentlessly dynamic operating circumstances.

Spontaneous Emergence of Positive Unintended Outcomes from Purposive Practical Coping

Freed from the shackles of purposeful goal-driven targets, pre-emptive purposive actions have the potential to generate unexpected but beneficial outcomes (Dreyfus, 1991) even though such 'goal-seeking' actions tend to be not sufficiently appreciated by social theorists (March, 1972). Yet, evidence shows that many lasting human accomplishments that we take so much for granted, are attributable to this kind of prospective purposive action. Thus, the invention of language, civil society, money and the emergence of medieval cities and so on, arose from the everyday practical coping actions of a multitude of people, none of whom intended or foresaw those eventual outcomes. These social institutions and structures arose out of practical frustrations: from coping with the implications of communication shortcomings (language), from needing to meet collective requirements (society), from enabling more efficient economic exchange (money) and from needing the convenience to trade and engage in commerce (medieval cities).

Adam Ferguson, an eighteenth-century contemporary of Adam Smith, for instance, points out that civil society as we know it is not the product of any deliberate design. Instead, 'Every step, every movement of the multitudes ... are made with equal blindness to the future; and nations stumble upon establishments, which are indeed the result of human action, but not the execution of any human design' (Ferguson, 1767/1966: 122, in Chia and Holt, 2009: 25). Modern civil society with its structures and institutions is the aggregative product of a multitude of everyday practical coping actions. The same insight applies to the myriad technical and social solutions we have found to alleviate our human condition. Most of our outstanding social and economic accomplishments began from lowly origins (*pudenda origo*) rather than from ambitious plans. The same applies for effective organisational strategy-making; from the bottom-up and not top-down.

Reality is too dynamic, complex, unknowable and interdependent for us to be able to survey and predict how our actions in evolving circumstances will play out. This is what a processual worldview emphasises. But it doesn't mean we can't cope or even profit from the situations faced on a day-to-day basis. Far from it. From a processual perspective, 'unowned' change is positively construed as a valuable source of potential for exploitation. It may require the need for coping with, but it also can yield unanticipated benefits provided we are able to harmonise our actions with the momentum and flow of events and circumstances to capitalise on them. As such, a keen awareness of context, momentum and situational tendencies is critical in enabling timely and impactful actions to be undertaken with an economy of effort as part of effective strategising.

Society/Social Orders Comprise Bundles of Social Practices Contain a Modus Operandi

From a processual worldview, it is historically shaped, sociocultural *practices* that provide the foundational basis for ordering our lives, making the fluxing context more manageable and liveable. Society is only able to function effectively when there is a 'workable level of certainty' (Weick, 1979: 6) and hence predictability. Without this regularity and predictability, the conduct of human affairs and the benefits arising from social and economic exchange would not be possible. Social orders, institutions and organisations are thus necessary for regulating the conduct of social life. But from a processual worldview, these social orders, structures and entities are no more than 'bundles' of established sociocultural practices (Schatzki, 2005).

These *sociocultural* practices 'bundles' aggregate from a multitude of effective everyday practical coping actions. They are refined and retained over time because of their demonstrated effectiveness in regularly delivering desirable outcomes in a wide variety of environmental circumstances. Over time, such practices congeal, spread and morph into internalised yet unwritten 'recipes' for action; they contain a modus operandi drawn upon – often unthinkingly – by members of a collective in response to environmental challenges and situational needs.

Practices are the 'building blocks' of societies, institutions and organisations. These social entities exist and persist only in so far as the bundles of practices that constitute them continue to be enacted and re-enacted on an ongoing basis. However, it is human tendency to forget the essentially precarious nature of social entities, held together as they are only through consensual, continued enactment of established practices. A processual worldview reminds us that social institutions such as organisations and common constructs such as 'the market', 'the environment' and so on, simply refer to bundles of practices. A 'firm' is no more than the 'firming-up' of a bundle of such practices; relax the practices and the firm becomes 'infirmed!'

Sociocultural practices as collectively shared ways of doing things are transmitted through practical demonstration and emulation rather than con- sciously taught. They are acquired in the same manner a child learns to mimic adult gestures and mannerisms through observing others. Children imitate not by learning abstract 'models' but by observing the habitual actions (hexis) of others: 'Body *hexis* speaks directly to the motor function, in the form of a pattern of postures . . . a way of walking, a tilt of the head, facial expressions' (Bourdieu, 1977: 87, emphasis original).

Practices serve to regulate collective behaviours and to delimit the range of socially acceptable responses to situations encountered. They contain 'schemes of perception, thought and action' (Bourdieu, 1990: 54) that persist over time and yet at the same time, they allow for wide flexibility in application according to the circumstances faced. They contain a patterned consistency or modus operandi that shapes collective predispositions and responses among members so that they largely respond in similar predictable ways. This same situation applies to members of an organisations.

As maintained in Section 1, an organisation's modus operandi ensures a relative consistency in its 'strategic' responses to circumstances arising. Consequently, effective strategic performance outcomes can be attained even though there isn't any explicitly articulated strategy or strategic plan. From a processual worldview, modus operandi explains and accounts for why *SiP* is crucial in shaping an organisation's strategy-making efforts.

ILLUSTRATIVE EXAMPLE: RED VENTURES – MAKE EVERY MOMENT COUNT

As reported by the *New York Times* (Smith, 2021), Ric Elias is the founder of a $10B corporation – Red Ventures – comprising a portfolio of branded media companies sharing a modus operandi centred on adaptability. The hallmark of strategising practices in businesses in the Red Ventures group is that 'everything is written in pencil', on the basis that the world is changing at a pace that is too fast to do otherwise and remain effective. With pride, Elias observes, 'I think we're a 20-year-old company that still is figuring out what we're going to be'. Elias was one of the passengers of the 'miracle on the Hudson', the plane crash immortalised in the movie Sully. The experience affected him profoundly and led him to advise 'live with urgency and make every moment count'. Defining practices as 'what you tolerate', many expected top-down practices of strategic management were deemed incompatible with the focus on flexibility and change in Red Venture businesses.

For example, setting of top-down financial targets is viewed as both arbitrary and dangerous given the dynamism of reality. The espoused rationale is that when targets are set, employees at all levels will take actions required to hit them rather than maximise the opportunities inherent in any situation, rarely seeking to change targets to more appropriate aspirations should the situation evolve. These eventualities don't live up to the expectation of 'making every moment count'. Instead, employees at all levels are encouraged to focus on doing the best work that the situation allows, and by striving to be great at actions taken in a timely way, to trust that appropriate accomplishments will follow. Creative experimentation and investment in new operational infrastructure, innovative technology and training are actively encouraged as a source of improved results and strategic growth from the 'bottom up'. Living by these principles, Red Ventures continues to evolve, grow and attain sector-leading profitability without many hallmarks of a conventional top-down goal-setting approach.

The axiom 'making every moment count' intimates a need to stay 'in the present'; to be observationally sensitised to goings-on in the here-and-now.

Effective Practical Coping Begins with Observational Fidelity

Prospective purposive responses begin with *observational fidelity* – a refined sensitivity to the minutiae of goings-on in the here-and-now of situations encountered. Observational fidelity describes the ability to see 'purely'; for detecting the slightest of changes going on within and without an organisation that may have implications for the organisation's future. Observational fidelity is a prerequisite for the cultivation of discriminative attunement (Gibson, 1979); the ability to detect the finest of 'differences that make a difference' (Bateson, 1972: 453). Like a needle on a vinyl record, the smallest of perturbations detected by seasoned practitioners can intimate vital information that feeds into an effective assessment of a situation encountered that guides appropriate responses. Through extended experiences of dwelling in a specific setting, a practitioner's sensitivity to contextual happenings and the granularity of their situational observations naturally increases. As observational fidelity is progressively attained and discriminative attunement refined, the practitioner becomes more nuanced in selecting appropriate, timely responses to emergent situations, improving the likelihood of realising satisfactory outcomes from the complex flow of events. Observational fidelity plays a key role in human evolution.

Within evolutionary theory, a processual worldview upholds the Bergsonian idea of *creative evolution* (Bergson, 1911/1998) instead of the more deterministic Darwinian notion of 'natural selection' as the basis of evolution. Rather than the more passive, Darwinian 'adaptation' to the environment suggested, humans in particular are capable of a proactive 'exaptation' (Gould and Vrba, 1982). Exaptation defines a creative capacity for extracting and repurposing any situational affordance detected into an advantage-gaining moment that enhances survival and growth. This capacity for creatively harnessing aspects of reality and fashioning it to suit our particular needs is what has elevated the status of human life to what it is today. As such, exaptation is made possible because of prolonged close-quarter engagement with a specific environment so that the necessary discriminative attunement needed for sensing and exploiting the affordances proffered is gradually cultivated.

Broadly, environmental excitations solicit our attention and raise awareness of the possible affordances the environment proffers us (Gibson, 1979). This, in turn, prompts a purposive coping response that draws on the collective repository of practices previously internalised, to produce a desired outcome. The perceived degree of success of such responses is subsequently registered and fed into a refined repertoire of practices shared with others. The result is an aggregation and congealing of these effective coping actions into established practices containing a modus operandi that serves as a heuristic guide for dealing with similar situations encountered in future. This same effect happens in organisational strategising even though it is often overlooked in the designing of formal strategy processes.

Environmental affordances describe the milieu of possibilities available to an actor deeply immersed in a setting. But what an environment affords depends on the circumstances faced and the capabilities of the actors themselves. Water, for example, may afford drinking to humans but not respiration. The surface of water can support some insects, but not people (Gibson, 1979). In short, exploitation of an affordance requires discernment of crucial differences and an understanding of which affordances are relevant, potentially valuable and worth exploiting. The 'education of attention' to particular aspects of the environment that hold potential value to the perceiver is thus crucial for the effective exploitation of affordances. This is what discriminative attunement associated with observational fidelity entails. Socialisation plays an important role in transmitting the shared discriminative capacity within a specific community. This is how and why, unlike most of us, members of an Inuit community, for example, can detect and differentiate between some forty-two different types of snow, understand their implications and respond accordingly (Krupnik et al., 2010). For them, this capability is a matter of survival.

From a processual worldview, it is expected that discriminative attunement to environmental affordances will vary between organisations in a path-dependent way. Idiosyncratic practices for detecting and appraising environmental affordances play a critical role in shaping distinctive 'strategic' choices arising from strategic assessments. And, to varying degrees, these choices influence the outcomes realised from the flow of events in which the organisation is embedded. It follows that individual or organisational activities resulting in a more refined discriminative attunement will naturally create more potential for exploitation for the organisation. From this processual worldview, therefore, discriminative attunement is a crucial prerequisite for the kind of sensing needed for effective strategy-making.

ILLUSTRATIVE HISTORICAL EXAMPLE: THE EUROPEANS IN NEW ENGLAND

When the first European settlers arrived in the New England region of America they began cultivating the land with local crops. As they were new to the climate, they were unclear about the effects of seasonal changes and sought advice from the Native Americans who had been farming the territory for hundreds of years. The settlers were keen on growing maize and were told to plant their corn when the 'oak leaves were the size of a squirrel's ear' (Scott, 1998: 311). Scott points out that embedded in this piece of peculiar local advice was a keenly attuned observation of the natural flow of events occurring in the New England spring. He writes: 'For Native Americans, it was this *orderly* succession of, say, the skunk cabbage appearing, the willows beginning to leaf, the red-winged blackbird returning, and the first hatch of the mayfly that provided a readily observable calendar of spring.' While the timing of these events might happen earlier or later in any particular year, the 'sequence of the events was never violated' (Scott, 1998: 312).

The Native Americans had, through their finely honed discriminative attunement, registered fine differences in the changing seasons and learnt how to maximise yield of crops by tracking the signs of nature to pick the right moments for successful cultivation. The cumulative aggregation of astute observational practices enabled the Native Americans to succeed in their cultivation endeavours in changeable circumstances.

In this section we highlighted the practical value of prospective, purposive action as goal-seeking rather than as a goal-driven activity. We explored how such oftentimes prospective purposive coping actions can generate positive unintended consequences of benefit to society (such as the un-designed emergence of language, medieval cities and civil society). We examined how these practical coping actions draw from 'bundles' of sociocultural practices containing a modus operandi that is shared through tacit processes of social-isation. Finally, we show how such sociocultural practices begin with obser-vational fidelity involving the continuous refining of discriminative attunement to facilitate the detection of environmental affordances and this is what enables effective coping or even profit to accrue from the unfolding situations encountered.

4 A Process-Practices Perspective on Strategic and Dynamic Capabilities

> Habitus, (or *modus operandi*) as systems of durable, transposable dispositions . . . generate and organize practices . . . (It) is the source of these strings of 'moves' which are . . . strategies without being the product of a strategic intention
>
> (Bourdieu, 1990: 53–62).

In this section, we:

- Recapitulate main theoretical premises of the resource-based view (RBV) and Dynamic Capabilities (DCs) approach to strategic management.
- Explain the grounding of strategic and dynamic capabilities in organ-isational practices from a *processual* perspective.
- Explain how generic coping capabilities arise from the human/environ-ment nexus.
- Emphasise the importance of discriminative attunement (the making of fine differentiations) for developing strategic/dynamic capabilities.
- Review and reinterpret the Teecian 'sensing-seizing-transforming' model of dynamic capability from a *processual* perspective.

Organisational activities that generate improvements in circumstances or temporary advantage that provides leverage over competitive rivals are essen-tially strategic acts. Even the smallest, seemingly innocuous, advantage-gaining acts can be vital in ensuring the viability of an organisation as a social and/or economic unit because of their possible 'snowballing' effect. Such strategic acts are guided by an organisation's internalised capabilities: the practised ability to sense, select and mobilise resources and know-how to achieve a required threshold level of performance. How such strategising acts link resources, context and demands together to generate a competitive advan-tage has been a much-researched question in the strategic management literature (Porter, 1984; Ghemawat, 1986; Barney, 1991; Peteraf, 1993; Burgelman et al., 2018; Mackay et al., 2023).

Proponents of the resource-based view (RBV) argue that an organisation's competitive strategy should focus on systematically exploiting its distinctive features such as its unique resources and capabilities (Wernerfelt, 1984; Barney, 1991; Peteraf, 1993). Differences in capabilities and resources available to an organisation help explain variations in strategic choices and outcomes among competitive rivals (Miller, 2003). An organisation outperforming its rivals in the competitive arena is said to be effectively exploiting its competitive advantage (for not-for-profit organisations, this means outperforming rivals for funding and attention). From an RBV perspective, organisations achieve their competitive advantage by generating outcomes that are:

(V)aluable to stakeholders

(R)are – demand exceeds supply

(I)nimitable – hard to copy effectively

(N)on-substitutable, that is, the same outcomes can't be produced by other
   means

This VRIN framework, for identifying how competitive advantage is achieved, was proposed by Barney (1991: 106–12) as part of RBV. An RBV assumes that differences in competitive advantage arise because stocks of resources and organisational capabilities are inevitably *heterogeneously* distributed among competing organisations. Performance differentials – or even organisational survival – depend on an organisation adopting a unique strategy that secures VRIN outcomes.

The challenge for RBV research, however, is how to explain the heterogeneous distribution of resource and capabilities among competing organisations. This is the reason for Teece et al. (1997) introducing their seminal concept of 'dynamic capabilities' (DCs) to help explain how organisations sustain competitive advantage over their rivals. For Teece et al. (1997: 516), DC refers to an organisation's capacity to successfully 'integrate, build, and reconfigure internal and external competences to address rapidly changing environments'. This capacity arises from an organisation's specific history and path-dependent activities involving the evolution of a unique set of idiosyncratic processes, routines and capabilities. Each organisation inevitably follows its own distinctive pathway of development so that a unique profile of idiosyncratic capabilities ensues. This explains why organisational capabilities are heterogeneously distributed. When effectively deployed, DC results in beneficial performance outcomes for an organisation particularly in dynamically changing circumstances.

ILLUSTRATIVE EXAMPLE: LVMH

Louis Vuitton Moet Hennessey (LVMH) is a luxury consumer goods corporation that achieved €64.2bn turnover in 2021 (www.lvmh.com). Over the decades it has developed through organic growth punctuated by mergers and acquisitions and has built a 'house of brands' that is trusted and prized by an affluent, global consumer base. Bulgari was one of those acquisitions in 2011, a process through which their head of group, Francesco Trapani, was appointed president of Watchmaking and Jewellery at LVMH. Commenting on the role of unique histories in luxury and super-premium purchases (Analis, 2012), he noted that for super-premium products, consumers are heavily influenced by the history of the brand. He notes that this is why organisations such as LVMH are increasingly spending time and money on telling the public their history and the different stages of that history. Their unique stories imbue their products with a character and style that is unique and that isn't available elsewhere, and which must be maintained through the highest, quality experience-in-use of the product. He observes that clients distinguish between brands with twenty years of experience and brands with 150 years of experience, so brands with long histories gear their product launches to the past – they RE-launch products that are more interesting than mere new products. He notes that this inspires the organisation to make significant investment every year in developing new materials to launch new products that draw on their rich, inimitable histories.

Mr Trapani's comments show how LVMH leverages historically accrued assets and capabilities through well-refined marketing narratives and continual investment in product improvement. This is done whilst continuing to seek out new acquisition targets to join the house of brands, recognising that, in the eyes of their target customers, there is no substitute for history.

Implied in Teece et al.'s (1997) claim is the view that DC – accrued as part of an organisation's unique historical journey – is unavoidably idiosyncratic and hence heterogeneously distributed amongst rivals. Eisenhardt and Martin (2000: 1118) however disagree. They insist that DCs are shared 'best practices', comprising 'simple, experiential rules' and 'rational heuristics' common to all competing organisations. Peteraf et al. (2013: 1389) note that these 'two mutually exclusive approaches for framing dynamic capabilities' – between idiosyncratic and common profiles – have shaped subsequent research of DC as a strategic management concept.

In recent attempts at clarification, Teece (2014: 338) has reiterated that DCs are essentially idiosyncratic and 'non-routine' in character. Whilst acknowledging the existence of rules, routines and heuristics, Teece nevertheless points to the crucial role that entrepreneurial activity plays in enabling *sui generis* (unique) responses to organisational circumstances faced (Teece, 2012). Such entrepreneurial responses point to the fact that DCs are tied to deep 'enterprise-specific roots' and so cannot be 'easily imitated by other organisations that did not and cannot share this history and . . . corporate culture' (Teece, 2014: 333). LVMH is a case in point. In fact the historical grounding of DC is often so complex that 'the organisation itself, let alone its competitors, does not understand them' (Teece et al., 1997: 525).

Teece's arguments point to the essentially tacit nature of DC as capabilities that resist simple codification and explicit articulation. To help clarify, Teece (2007: 1320) points to the qualities of 'sensing', 'seizing' and 'transforming' opportunities in the extant environment as core micro-foundational elements of an organisation's DC. For him, this is what explains 'superior long term financial performance' of an organisation. Yet, Teece does not elaborate further on where this sensing, seizing and transforming capacity comes from or how it is developed within an organisation.

Notwithstanding Eisenhardt and Martin's (2000) disagreements, Teece's portrayal of DC as idiosyncratic, historically forged and infused with non-routine entrepreneurial capacities is now widely accepted in the strategy literature. Yet, even with this clarification, the concept of DC has been criticised for its lack of practical application potential (Zeng and Mackay, 2019). Moreover, from a processual perspective, Nayak et al. (2019: 281) note that Teece and his associates appear to be struggling to 'articulate a tacit, non-analytic, experientially based way of explaining effective adaptive action'. For them, Teece's efforts to explain DC are hindered by a lack of awareness of the 'practice turn' vocabulary. Accordingly, it is insights from this 'practice turn' underpinned by a processual worldview that can cast fresh light onto the phenomenon of DC.

Strategic/Dynamic Capabilities Are Grounded in Shared Organisational Practices

In their overview of the contemporary strategy literature, Mackay et al. (2023: 5–9) note that over recent decades strategy research has expanded from an early focus on the *content* of strategy (Ansoff, 1975; Porter, 1980; Wernerfelt, 1984) to strategy *processes* (Mintzberg, 1973; Pettigrew, 1973, 1992; Mintzberg and Waters, 1985) to a sociological examination of *strategy-as-practice* (SAP) in recent years (Whittington, 1996; Johnson et al., 2003; Kohtamäki et al., 2022).

In the latter case, there has been an attempt to draw from the 'practice turn' in social theory (Schatzki et al., 2001) to expand understanding of strategy and strategy-making.

These changing emphases reflect the shift in focus away from macro-economic analyses to the micro-activities, interactions, and practices of strategy-making as an ongoing process. Whilst SAP is clearly a move in this direction, there remains scope to deepen understanding and value of strategy-making by adopting a processual worldview to ideas expressed in the SAP literature (Bourdieu, 1990; Chia, 2004; Kohtamäki et al., 2022; MacKay et al., 2021) and by emphasising practices as the site for capabilities development.

As elaborated previously, adopting a processual worldview implies that practices are collectively shared ways of doing things; they contain a modus operandi and are congealed aggregations of a multitude of effective practical coping actions taken in situ. Practices contain patterned regularities for dealing with issues encountered and carry the impulse of history, habit and tradition. Yet, practices contain sufficient flexibility for specific application in context. And practices facilitate the tacit acquisition of skill and capabilities, including for DCs.

Practices ensure that in situ coping actions draw from historically accumulated know-how to address the present in preparation for the future. This developmental profile resonates with a paths-positions-possibilities reading of DC as originally proposed by Teece et al. (1997). DCs as internalised organisational practices display a processual quality in that each successful adaptive response feeds into, modifies and fine-tunes established practices and with it the organisational modus operandi in preparation for the next encounter. Hence, each coping act is a continuation of 'the past which gnaws into the future and which swells as it advances' (Bergson, 1911/1998: 2). As Teece (2014) notes, such ongoing refining activity takes on an entrepreneurial character, exhibiting a degree of creative 'exaptation' (cf. last section's discussion of exaptation). This processual framing explains how an organisation's DC develop idiosyncratically through ongoing refinement of practices via extended close-quarter contact with an extant environment.

A modus operandi is detectable in organisational practices, ineluctably shaped by sociocultural forces throughout an organisation's history of operational experiences and shaping the sensing, seizing and transforming activities proposed by Teece (2007). A modus operandi directs the focus of attention, refines discriminative attunement and enables the mobilisation of appropriate coping responses to specific situations apprehended. By so doing it ensures a 'strategic' consistency in organisational responses over time that are historically shaped, idiosyncratic and unique.

Modus operandi is also intimated in professional practices and vocational occupations; for example, the 'practice' of acupuncture or a medical 'practice' (Barnes, 2001). A highly proficient practitioner is acutely attuned to the methods, protocols, and predispositions of their profession and the sensitivities, traditions and context in which they are embedded or associated. The effective practitioner realises that they are not at liberty to 'do' as they like but instead are required to work within the tacit constraints of a shared modus operandi. What we call a 'profession' therefore is made up of sanctioned practices and protocols to which the professional is obliged to adhere closely to. Yet, in the specifics of each individual circumstance, the proficient practitioner is able to exercise discretion in the manner and choice of practice combinations to be deployed. This predisposition is similar to DC.

As the underlying source of DC, an organisation's modus operandi enables members sufficient flexibility to display all the '"reasonable," "common sense," behaviours' as they go about their business without any unnecessary 'extravagance' (Bourdieu, 1990: 54) yet with the capacity and even propensity for 'regulated improvisations' (Bourdieu, 1990: 57) when faced with unexpected or unforeseen circumstances. Modus operandi ensures the necessary built-in flexibility of responsiveness that explains what Teece et al. (1997) are driving at in their conception of DC. The Teecian triad of 'sensing, seizing and transforming' is thus a result of tacitly acquired organisational practices, comprising a refined discriminative attunement to subtle environmental changes, and a unique modus operandi that enables the effective mobilisation of appropriate strategic responses to environmental affordances. DC, as such, describe the similar qualities of 'mastery' we often see displayed in competitive sports and games that require both situational sensitivity, disciplined application and innovative moves in specifically situated circumstances.

ILLUSTRATIVE EXAMPLE: CAPABILITY DEVELOPMENT IN CHESS MASTERY

The philosopher Hubert Dreyfus (2002: 368–72) provides a 'practice-based' understanding of skills acquisition and capability development in mastering the game of chess. The novice learns basic rules and principles, which are to be mechanically followed. The advanced beginner starts to learn to think ahead to avoid problematic positions and create issues for opponents. With more accumulated experience, the competent player sets aside the 'detached rule-following stance of the beginner' and realises that there are a 'vast number of situations differing from each other in subtle, nuanced ways'. To the extent that there is no exhaustive list of what to do in every possible situation, coping now for the competent player becomes anxiety-ridden rather than tedious; the performer becomes emotionally involved in performing his/her tasks.

At the next stage of proficiency, adherence to rules and principles gives way to a capacity for situational discriminations and measured responses. Action becomes more spontaneous and less stressful as the performer simply sees what needs to be done rather than having to consciously deliberate and decide by any rule-based calculative procedure. Finally, at the stage of mastery, the expert not only sees what needs to be done, thanks to a vast repertoire of situational discriminations (s)he has internalised through practice, but also has developed the necessary flexibility required to respond appropriately to novel circumstances not previously envisaged. These subtle and refined capabilities distinguish the expert from the proficient performer, the competent player and the novice.

How Capabilities Are Developed through the Organisation/Environment Nexus

As intimated in the previous section, humans actively select promising aspects of their immediate environment that afford possibilities for enhancing their life situation. Consequently, what we find 'out there' in the environment depends very much on our immediate concerns and preoccupations: when hungry we seek out opportunities to relieve our hunger; when trying to evade danger, we seek a safe hiding place; when weary we seek shelter and resting place. The 'environment', therefore, is not simply some singular pre-existing objective reality. Rather what it affords to a perceiver depends on the needs and preoccupations of the latter. The same situation applies in the case of the organisation/environment nexus; what the environment affords an organisation depends on the needs, concerns and capabilities of the organisation itself.

But how can an organisation know which of the myriad environmental affordances to respond to in order to act 'strategically'? This requires an examination of the organisation/environment nexus. We can begin by considering the characteristics of environmental affordances. Firstly, environmental affordances have an objective quality about them: 'a fruit says "Eat me", water says "Drink me", a handle says "grasp me" and thunder says "Fear me"' (Koffka, 1935: 7). There is a 'demand' or 'invitation character' about the extant environment that, through discriminative attunement, we can detect the possibilities proffered. But the possibilities afforded by an environment may differ significantly for each actor immersed in it. For example, to members of a society with a developed habit of sitting, a terrestrial surface that is horizontal, flat, rigid, and knee-high automatically affords the opportunity for sitting. But to an aboriginal community more accustomed to squatting than sitting, there is no equivalent perception of such an affordance and hence no attempt to make use of it. Consequently, environmental affordances, though objectively existing and abundant, are nevertheless still relative and subjected to perception (Gibson, 1979).

In organisational strategy, therefore, perceptions of affordances are invariably influenced by broader sociocultural outlooks as well as the organisation's own history, traditions and experiences. This is why organisations develop different capabilities and why heterogeneity of capabilities is inevitable. According to a processual worldview, perception is not simply about passively registering what exists 'out there', but rather about a more active process of detecting subtle differences in the extant environment and then formulating possibilities for appropriate response (Gibson, 1979). This is where previously established shared practices shaped by the aggregation of past practical coping actions play a crucial role in guiding response.

So, while the capacity for discriminative attunement enables the detection of minute differences that intimate an opportunity for exploitation, we turn to collectively shared practices containing an internalised modus operandi to enable us to 'seize' and 'transform' those sensed opportunities into a useful advantage. Capabilities are developed from a combination of these two aspects; discriminative attunement and the application of shared practices containing a modus operandi. Discriminative attunement directs attention to facets of the environment that afford potential strategic opportunities for exploitation and practised capability is crucial in extracting strategic advantage from the circumstance faced.

What we call DC then, is a result of the combination of this finely honed sensitivity and the associated internalised ability and coping skills to respond accordingly. By harmonising organisational actions with the natural bent of evolving environmental circumstances it is then possible to efficiently benefit from the flow of events in a way that economises on effort and enhances survival and growth potential (Jullien, 1999; Ingold, 2000). This is how competitive advantage is achieved.

Blending practically accrued know-how and wisdom with fresh experimental attempts, guided by modus operandi, to meet the needs of novel situations encountered, results in the routine-entrepreneurial mix Teece (2012) proposes as constitutive of DC. Prior collective experiences inevitably orient an organisation and its members in their present and future engagements without necessarily determining exactly how they will respond in situ since such responses are not merely reflexive 'effects', nor are they necessarily deliberately intentional or conscious. Instead, an organisation's collective reading of environmental excitations evokes quasi-patterned responses, attenuated by the history of its experiences, in a manner which reflects its idiosyncratic capabilities and practices.

Strategic 'Sensing' through Discriminative Attunement

Strategic sensing requires a requisite level of observational fidelity to establish accurately what the extant environment proffers in terms of possibilities and limitations. What Teece (2007) called 'sensing' points to the capacity for detecting very subtle but significant differences that make a difference. This discriminative attunement is the result of striving to attain a pure, pristine seeing 'unwarped by the sophistication of theory' (Whitehead, 1929/1978: 295). The point of this pure seeing is not to allow the intellect and preconceptions 'distort' our perception of what is actually going on in the world of affairs; observational fidelity is crucial. The value of this kind of pure seeing for aiding effective strategic decision-making has been unequivocally emphasised by the founders of several successful Japanese conglomerates (Matsushita, 2002; Inamori, 2014), amongst others.

As pointed out previously, the perceiving of an affordance entails detection of ever finer-grained differences that make a difference in the extant environment (Bateson, 1972: 453) that offers possibilities for productive responses. Take the practice of wine tasting for instance. A novice wine taster may only be able to distinguish between drinks based on easily observable visual attributes such as colour. But a connoisseur can detect much finer differences corresponding to specific grapes, regions and even the year harvested. Through years of practice in tasting wine, following hallowed traditions, small subtle differences that exist in the chemical signature of different wines are detected and become ever more distinguishable by the expert. This capacity for discriminative attunement is a result of the connoisseur investing extensive amounts of time sampling, making mistakes and refining their discriminative capabilities. Wine connoisseurs are also required to forego activities that might diminish accrued capabilities, such as drinking tea or coffee (as they interfere with palette).

Across all categories of practical mastery, we note an inextricable relationship between immersed experience, discriminate attunement and refined capabilities. Thus:

> Experienced drivers can easily perceive whether the gaps opening up in moving traffic will allow them to merge or switch lanes while experienced listeners can distinguish the cellos from the violins and the clarinets from the oboes and expert radiologists can distinguish a cancerous spot from normal breast tissue on a mammogram (Adolph and Kretch, 2015: 131).

Detection of such fine differences and emergent possibilities is a consequence of what the evolutionary psychologist Eleanor Gibson (1997: 25) describes as the prospective activity of extracting information from 'previously vague impressions' (Gibson and Gibson, 1955: 34) through finely differentiating one situation from another. This 'close-reading' of what the environment or situation proffers profoundly contributes to the development of generic strategic capabilities associated with DC and in particular, the sensing, seizing and transforming of opportunities available.

This same capacity for staying close to the ground and attuned to operational realities, detecting nuanced situational affordances and seizing opportunities arising, led to Japanese manufacturing superiority in the 1980s.

ILLUSTRATIVE EXAMPLE: JAPANESE MANUFACTURING STRATEGY IN THE 1980S

In the 1980s Japanese manufacturers of cars and electronics began to dominate world markets based on superior quality and efficiency of outputs. Competitors engaged in a frantic search for the 'secrets' of Japanese manufacturing success. Concepts of manufacturing excellence such as Just-in-Time approaches and Total Quality Management were touted and fervently adopted by competing corporations around the world. However, overlooked in this enthusiastic rush were the underlying operational attitudes, predispositions and sociocultural practices unique to the Japanese that enabled advanced manufacturing methods to be pursued in a socially acceptable way. Transplanting Japanese manufacturing techniques into non-Japanese corporations produced highly mixed results and subsequently widespread disillusionment.

This epoch shows how operational capabilities nurtured within a specific set of sociocultural circumstances can lead to inimitable superior performance in a globally competitive manufacturing environment. In *Japanese Manufacturing Techniques: Nine Hidden Lessons in Simplicity*, Schonberger (1982) attempted to describe features of the manufacturing superiority that had become so evident to the rest of the world. But the supposed 'secrets' highlighted were criticised by the Japanese manufacturers themselves, who regarded their culturally shaped intolerance for imperfection (their modus operandi) as the enduring feature underpinning manufacturing superiority (Shingo, 1985).

To Shigeo Shingo, a consultant figure central to development of Toyota's much lauded production systems, popularised Western accounts missed the true essence of the competitive advantage of Japanese manufacturing approaches. The most crucial aspect Shingo identified was a Japanese cultural predisposition for pure seeing and for the relentless perfecting of action. Encapsulated in the term '*kaizen*', which really means 'continuous self-criticism' this innate drive for 'cleansing oneself' intellectually, to enable pure seeing and hence self-cultivation through the perfecting of action, inspired methods such as SMED (Single Minute Exchange of Dies), Poke-Yoke (Fail-Safe Systems) and Zero Defects (Shingo, 1985). The SMED underpinned Just-in-Time delivery systems, enabling companies like Toyota to compete successfully against their Western counterparts. However, terms such as Just-in-Time were never part of the vocabulary employed by the Japanese manufacturers; they were Western conceptualisations of what they observed arising organically in Japanese factories.

For many years, the operational capability of being able to flexibly and rapidly respond to unexpected and shifting demands gave Japanese manu-facturing a major strategic advantage in a turbulent and rapidly changing business environment.

A Processual Understanding of Dynamic Capabilities

Integral to historically shaped practices and the modus operandi contained therein, capabilities begin with observational fidelity and the subsequent devel-opment of discriminative attunement for guiding coping responses. Through modus operandi, a distillation of complex, unique historical experiences and practical wisdom is made available to organisational members as a basis for responding to situational exigencies in a patterned, socially acceptable way. Discriminative attunement underpins 'sensing' capacity in an organisation, and modus operandi guides practical coping responses; the latter drawing from a repository of shared practices to 'seize' and 'transform' situational affor-dances to achieve a competitive advantage (Nayak et al., 2019).

From a processual worldview, therefore, tacitly shared practices in an organisation provide the foundational basis for DC. Yet, it is crucial to remember that DC is not some permanent attribute or fixture. The assumption that once accrued DC will endure is misplaced, and overlooks the dynamic nature of the capabilities. Constant refinement and re-fashioning of appropri-ate responses is needed because of continuous and intense close-quarter engagement with an environment that is ever-changing. This is what embra-cing a processual worldview entails; accepting that change and changing circumstances are inevitable, and that it is erroneous to simply assume that what follows will be like what has come before. Prior success is no guarantee of future performance outcomes or success in analogous situations (O'Reilly and Tushman, 2008). As with any capability, if DC aren't maintained through constant adjustment of practice then effectiveness may atrophy over time or as knowledgeable personnel leave an organisation (Winter, 2003). These considerations imply a need for continual refinement of practices and modus operandi to maximise the potential of DC to be effectively deployed in the multitude of situations encountered. An attitude of embracing the ever-new and as-yet-unthought is a prerequisite for DC.

ILLUSTRATIVE EXAMPLE: RELATIVITY SPACE

Mackay et al. (2023) use the entrepreneurial journey of Relativity Space to illustrate the idiosyncratic nature of the development of strategic and dynamic capabilities. In 2015, Tim Ellis and Jordan Noone left their comfortable technologist jobs in prominent space industry organisations to form Relativity Space. They did so on a hunch that it was possible to disrupt the space industry by using novel digital production systems to manufacture rockets 'in days rather than years'. This bold leap of faith was enabled by their shared sensing of the possibilities presented by unfolding technology trajectories in 3D printing, artificial intelligence, and autonomous robotics; and emerging commercial demand from governments, commercial enterprises and space tourism for space launch payload capacity. When they formed Relativity Space however, the necessary technologies weren't yet available at the required scale.

What followed were years of cycling between persuading funders of technical and commercial viability, and using funds raised to develop and demonstrate technological progress, in order to attract more funders for the next phase and so on. Early in its journey, Relativity Space created the world's largest 3D metal printers – an attention-grabbing breakthrough. In subsequent years, complementary digital rocket design and manufacturing capabilities were nurtured to establish full operational viability. The result was demonstrated capacity to create rockets significantly faster and cheaper than their competitors. From the earliest insider's sense of opportunity in the flow of events, Relativity Space had become the second most valuable privately owned space company in the world even before the launch of its first rocket. The emergence of unique strategic and dynamic capabilities in Relativity Space's journey illustrates how continual development and renewal of practices enables challenges to be overcome and opportunities to be seized.

Much of what goes on in organisations making up what is called DC is rooted in unspectacular and seemingly innocuous but effective everyday practical coping actions taken to deal with exigencies faced. Through extended operational exposure, experienced practitioners – often unintentionally – acquire the necessary discriminative attunement to sense fine differences in, and perceive possibilities offered by, situations confronting them. Accompanying this finely honed capacity is an unconsciously acquired organisational modus operandi that guides their actions and reactions.

Discriminative attunement and responses guided by the modus operandi serve as foundational sources of tacit knowledge and practical wisdom arising from practical experience rather than abstract intellectual analyses. These alternative knowledge bases challenge the conventional privileging of 'thought' over 'action'. Because these capabilities and know-how are more tacit and hence less cognitively accessible, they are also harder to detect, grasp and explain than explicit, codified knowledge propounded in popular management texts. This renders critical an understanding of the potential of SiP in guiding and shaping organisational strategising, and in knowing how to work with DC. Through embracing a processual worldview, we can find new answers to enduring strategic questions relating to DC and how they help establish and maintain a competitive advantage for the organisation.

5 Reframing Strategic Change: A Process-Practices Perspective

> All real change is an indivisible change . . . If you imagine a change as being really composed of states . . . You have closed your eyes to reality.
>
> Bergson (1946/1992: 146–7)

In this section, we:

- Provide a summary of established views in which strategic change is understood in terms of disruptive and spectacular interventions triggered by deliberate strategic intent.
- Highlight the downsides associated with this penchant for dramatic strategic change interventions.
- Examine the potential benefits of an alternative processual approach to strategic change that is driven by the senses rather than the intellect.
- Reframe strategic change in terms of small, iterative coping adjustments that are aligned with the internal momentum of situations to achieve desired outcomes quietly and obliquely.

What would an SiP approach to strategic change, underpinned by a processual worldview, look and feel like? We begin with an observation of how change is construed in the substantialist worldview. Much of the current literature on strategic change paradoxically construes change as a transitive succession between otherwise discrete, stable states rather than as a genuinely continuous and interpenetrating process. In Section 2, we showed that this tendency is inextricably linked to the alphabetisation of Western thought. The theoretical physicist David Bohm points out that the English language's subject–verb–object grammatical structure in particular orients us to thinking in this successional way. This grammatical structure 'implies that all action arises in a separate entity, the subject, and that, in the case described by a tentative verb, this action crosses over the space between them to another separate entity, the object' (Bohm, 1980: 29) to produce a resultant effect. All change requires a stable, identifiable agent, the subject, acting on another object. Such a way of thinking becomes problematic when we consider a simple sentence like: 'it is raining'. What, asks Bohm is the 'It' that is doing the raining? The grammatical structure forces us to construe an imaginary 'it' as the subject initiating change. Unwittingly we have created a substantive and entitative understanding of reality.

These problems associated with the linguistic structuring of thought means that it is a real challenge to think in terms of genuine movement, emergence and changefulness in a non-substantialist way (Bergson, 1911/1998; Chia, 1999). Recent attempts at emphasising 'verbs' instead of 'nouns' (Bohm, 1980; Weick, 2009: 7) do go some way towards ameliorating our understanding of change processes. Yet, the prevailing tendency is still to fall back to a 'cinematographic method' (Bergson, 1911/1998) whereby strategic change is construed in discrete, successional and episodic terms. For example, Kurt Lewin's (1951) widely known 'unfreeze, change, refreeze' model of change, which presumes the linear, sequential replacement of one stable state by another, is still hugely popular in the strategic change literature (Kanter et al., 1992).

Underlying this substantialist approach to change is Newton's first Law of Motion which states: 'Every body continues in its state of rest or of uniform motion in a straight line, *except so far as it may be compelled by force to change that state*' (in Whitehead, 1926/1985: 58, our emphasis). In other words, not only is change linear and successional, but also without the imposition of an external force, no change can take place. Reality is essentially stable and substantial so that change has to be made to happen through external forces overcoming an internal inertia. Consequently, change is regarded as transient, intermittent, exceptional and externally initiated. The possibility that change may actually happen of its own accord, and that there may be 'unowned' forces of change (Rescher, 1996) – momentum and tendencies contained in the situations themselves – is not countenanced in the strategic change literature.

Much of the strategy literature and consultancy practices portray strategic change as a transient shifting of one otherwise stable state to another. Ford and Ford (1994: 773), for instance, describe change as taking place when 'one entity sequentially takes the place of or substitutes for a second'. This conjures images of a linear succession of discrete events replacing each other along a continuous timeline. Similarly, Van de Ven (1987: 331), insists that 'change without reference to an object is meaningless', that is, change is change of otherwise stable 'things'. From this substantialist worldview, no consideration is given to the converse notion that change may be primary and that objects, things and stable states are in fact abstractions from an 'unbroken and undivided whole movement' and that each 'thing' is only a 'relative invariant ... aspect of this movement' (Bohm, 1980: 47).

This residual substantialism persists even in more recent scholarly efforts on strategic change that emphasises thinking in terms of 'process' (e.g. Van de Ven and Poole, 1995; Pettigrew, 2012; Langley et al., 2013; Burgelman et al., 2018). Change continues to be construed as a 'process' that a substantial entity such as 'an organisation' undergoes. Process then, for these strategy theorists is a process of things. The idea that 'process' is reality (Whitehead, 1929/1978) is not countenanced. Consequently, despite the widespread use of terms like 'process', 'emergence' and 'evolution', such accounts continue to describe (strategic) change 'as though it were made of immobilities' (Bergson, 1946/ 1992: 145). This understanding of change as exceptional, externally imposed and frequently eye-catching derives from a substantialist worldview.

Within the mainstream press and academic literatures, strategic change initiatives are often portrayed in bold, disruptive and even dramatic terms. There is a penchant for the heroic and the spectacular in portraying strategic change interventions (Chia, 2014: 6). In warfare, politics, law and business the direct and heroic confrontational approach to effecting change to the status quo is eulogised (Jullien, 2000; Chia, 2014). Despite numerous reports of strategic change initiatives failing to realise anticipated gains, a commitment to understanding and approaching change directly and confrontationally continues to dominate theory and practice.

However, a genuinely processual reframing of reality fundamentally alters our understanding of change and our attitude and approach towards strategic change initiatives (Chia, 2014). As we have previously maintained, from this processual worldview, *'there are underneath the change no things which change ... there are movements, but there is no inert or invariable object which moves: movement does not imply a mobile'* (Bergson, 1946/1992: 147, emphasis original). According to this alternative processual worldview, pattern and order are no more than islands of relative stability in a churning sea of chaos. As such, the priorities and agenda for strategic change are vastly different. Instead of managing change by intervening to control and direct efforts towards pre-established goals, change is 'allowed' to happen naturally by 'letting go' (Chia, 2014: 13) and allowing it to find its own level and pace, much like the way spilled water flows and is allowed to arrive at its own equilibrium through opportunistic expansion, restless captures and unexpected conquests (Chia, 1999). But, this 'unowned' way of thinking strategic change is unnerving for many tied to a substantialist worldview. Yet, it offers many advantages in avoiding pitfalls of the direct and confrontational approach of attempting spectacular and dramatic change interventions.

ILLUSTRATIVE EXAMPLE: CONTINUOUS 'UNOWNED' CHANGE IN THE SCOTCH WHISKY INDUSTRY

The Scotch Whisky industry is worth £5.5bn annually to the UK economy. It is a sector built on 'patient capital', requiring the laying down of stocks (distilling and storing whisky in barrels) years in advance of them being ready for sale. This aging process allows the flavour and character of the liquid to mature, increasing the potential affordances and value of the whisky. Through minimal but learned interventions over the years as the whisky matures, the quality of the whisky stocks arising can be improved in a way that delivers unique attributes, sometimes decades later. Value arises from the impact of natural change processes refining the composition of the liquid in the barrel. Allowing the liquid to 'mature' is a critical aspect of whisky distillation. Organisational success in exploiting this potential depends on knowing when and how to manage and harvest the liquid, attuned to environmental conditions as diverse as climate change and consumer trends.

Reviewing the epoch 1945–present in the industry, MacKenzie et al. (2022) illustrate how – despite the common constraint of a slow, continual process of creating whisky stocks – the industry itself is continually evolving. The rise and fall of seemingly dominant players over the years is spurred by environmental forces such as global supply, international politics, mergers and acquisitions, and new market entrances from industry 'outsiders', bringing disruptive strategic logics unencumbered by sectoral expectations. This historical period shows the illusory nature of permanence and stability, and the value – to survival and profitability – of refined discriminative attunement, strategic change capacity and dynamic capabilities even in an industry characterised by slow 'unowned' changes.

Downsides of the Direct, Dramatic and Disruptive Approach to Strategic Change

> [T]he breathless rhetoric of planned transformational change, complete with talk of revolution, discontinuity, and upheaval, presents a distorted view of how successful change works
>
> (Weick, 2009: 229).

A natural consequence of embracing a substantialist worldview is the privileging of the primacy of atomistic entities and hence the notion of methodological individualism (von Mises, 1949/1998) within the social sciences – that is, an emphasis on the primacy, autonomy and importance of individuals, their actions, and their impact on outcomes. Within the strategic change literature, there is no shortage of change narratives crediting organisational successes to the 'heroic' interventions of individual CEOs whilst overlooking the role that unfolding circumstances and the contributions of others play in shaping eventual outcomes. Faith in individual agency to make exceptional 'heroic' interventions encourages – in words at least – adoption of ambitious, high-profile planned approaches to managing change. Received wisdom is that change interventions must be rapid, spectacular, disruptive and deliberately led; actions must be decisive, and if necessary, resistances forcibly overcome, so that the desired outcome can be successfully accomplished without hindrance. An abundant expenditure of energy, effort and resources may be involved in formulating and implementing such top-down strategic change initiatives.

Inspired by Lewinian thinking, much of the literature on strategic change accepts such a direct, disruptive approach as necessary for successful interventions. Many advocates of this approach insist that effective strategic change cannot happen gradually (Romanelli and Tushman, 1994) or take place in a piecemeal manner (Gersick, 1991), but must be rapid, disruptive and even revolutionary (Peters, 1989). Moreover, since thinking is assumed to precede action, talk of revolutionary paradigmatic shifts abound in the strategic change literature (Burgelman and Grove, 2007), reinforcing the widespread view that effective strategic change must be planned, spectacular and initiated from the top-down.

Through dramatic narratives, successful strategic change is often associated with the heroic interventions of top management. Bourgeois and Eisenhardt's (1988) study on CEO decision-making is a case in point, lionising the role of top management in making 'important' decisions such as the 'strategic repositioning' of an organisation to achieve a quick and spectacular turn-around of fortunes. Thus, the decisions and actions of individual CEOs are deemed to be singularly causal in realising organisational success (Burgelman and Grove, 2007; Jarzabkowski, 2008). This eulogising of 'visionary' CEO leaders, attributing them with almost super-human qualities, is arguably part of the narrative-making required to justify high salaries and bonuses.

There are notable problematic aspects of this direct and disruptive approach to strategic change. The single-minded pursuit of a particular change outcome can result in the overlooking of concerns and anxieties of those immediately affected, leading to longer-term unintended consequences (Merton, 1936). It can provoke 'elements of internal resistance, reticence or withdrawal of cooperation' that quietly undermine the change initiative itself (Chia, 2014: 15). Invariably, a high-profile intervention 'tears at the tissue of things and upsets their (internal) coherence' (Jullien, 2004: 54), creating disquiet and discord among those affected and disrupting the established harmony of things. It 'pits individuals against one another, forces comparison, generates rivalry and conflict, produces tension and destructive competition that ultimately creates "winners" and "losers"' (Chia, 2014: 16). It divides loyalties, forcing those affected to take sides so that their coping actions are ultimately aimed at self-preservation and survival rather than the collective good of the organisation.

Large-scale, high-profile strategic change initiatives, because they are concentrated at one moment and not another, are inevitably 'loud' and lacerating. They constitute explosive breaches of the harmony and natural rhythm of things. As such they tend to generate an unsettling effect. They 'radicalize action and carry it to its highest intensity' (Jullien, 2011: 65) as in the advent of a strike or a revolution. Consequently, while spectacular interventions may satisfy the penchant for drama and excitement, they are not necessarily the most efficacious and are often wasteful in terms of energy, effort and resources expended.

ILLUSTRATIVE EXAMPLE: THE UNINTENDED CONSEQUENCES OF LARGE-SCALE STRATEGIC CHANGE

Flyvbjerg's (1998) detailed analysis of a failed high-profile plan to limit the use of cars in the city centre of Aalborg, Denmark in the 1990s illustrates how large-scale change programmes can generate unexpected responses that eventually thwarted the intended aims of the project itself. Against a growing concern with increasing city-centre traffic congestion the scheme was conceived to limit the use of cars within the city. However, right from the point where the decision was made, various parties with vested interests including the police, town planning consultants, the business community, public travel agencies, trade unions, the local media and even the citizenry became politically involved. Conflict of priorities emerged between town planners and the bus company regarding the location and size of the bus terminal, deeply dividing the task force. Furthermore, local businesses that had retail outlets within the planned restricted precinct were concerned that without cars being allowed into the city-centre area their businesses would inevitably suffer. The Environmental Protection Agency raised their concerns about environmental hazards arising from the proposed construction of the bus terminal. Local residents also objected. They maintained that the authentic charms of the old shopping streets would be destroyed by these large-scale urban renewal changes. Cyclists were also concerned about the lack of adequate cycle paths for their safety.

Yet another source of conflict emerged from the planning council's decisions to ban all non-retail businesses such as banks, insurance companies and administrative offices from occupying the ground floor premises so as to preserve the charms of the old city-centre streets. Objections to this proposal that arose were fast and furious. These and many other unanticipated reactions to the large-scale planned changes to the city centre resulted in no less than eleven modifications before the initiative was finally implemented in a virtually unrecognizable form. Importantly, the planned changes implemented did not produce the outcomes intended. Instead, traffic increased by 8 per cent, road accidents involving cyclists rose by 40 per cent and noise levels and pollution rose to exceed international norms. There are genuine downsides to large-scale strategic change initiatives. It appears that the more dramatic and spectacular the strategic change initiative, the more likely it is that it generates subsequent unintended consequences that thwart its intended outcome.

A Process-Practices Approach to Strategic Change

As previously discussed, a processual worldview assumes that movement and change are fundamental so that 'immobility' (i.e. stable states) only describe 'the extreme limit of the slowing down of movement' (Bergson, 1903/1955: 43). Reality is a continuous unbroken movement and objects and entities are simply stabilised patterns abstracted from the totality of this flow much like the way we abstract the pattern of a whirlpool from otherwise flowing water (Bohm, 1980).

In theorising change, then, we need not presuppose an 'object' or something changing. Instead, as highlighted earlier, '*There are changes, but there are* underneath the changes no things which change: change has no need of support. There are movements, but there is no inert or invariable object which moves: movement does not imply a mobile" (Bergson, 1946/1992: 147, emphasis original). This way of thinking about movement, change and transformation is quite alien to mainstream portrayals of strategic change. Yet, it is entirely consistent with the revolutionary ideas of quantum theory that have prepared the ground for the new physics of our time.

Two crucial insights arise from this processual understanding of reality. Firstly, reality is always 'becoming' and the inexorable emergence of novelty are fundamental features of reality (Whitehead, 1929/1978: 30). 'Unowned' changes (Rescher, 1996) are always already going on of their own accord independent of human actions and interventions. Sensitive discernment of such ongoing changes inherent in the flow of reality provides the key to effective strategic change management, requiring cultivation of a keener sense of observation and an astute reading of trajectories and propensities contained in evolving situations. Secondly, situations encountered are impregnated by the history of past happenings so that the past, present and future interpenetrate and implicate one another; they 'continue each other in an endless flow' (Bergson, 1911/1998: 4). Changes flow seamlessly and oftentimes silently of their own accord.

Acknowledging the pervasiveness of such unowned processional changes always already taking place allows us to approach strategic change differently. Instead of assuming that external force is always required to effect change, the imperative becomes one of learning to astutely read the propensity of situations encountered and then mobilising the inner momentum contained therein to redirect it to one's advantage. Thus, strategic change is more about 'letting happen' (Chia, 2014) than about forcible, disruptive intervention. Timely, unobtrusive insertions into unfolding situations help redirect and channel latent momentum towards desired ends with minimal effort, oftentimes unnoticed. This modus operandi of strategic change is less likely to be obstructed and hence to evoke internal resistance.

From a processual perspective, strategic change is not about the jarring replacement of one stable state by another preferred one, nor is it necessarily disruptive, spectacular or dramatic. Instead, successful strategic changes are most commonly inconspicuous, seeming natural and interwoven with gradual, even imperceptible, improvements in everyday effectiveness of responses. The obsession with high-profile, large-scale change interventions blinds us to the transformational potential of 'unowned' sociocultural and operational change processes always already taking place in situ. An acute awareness of these situational propensities can facilitate the pre-emptive fashioning of subtle, nuanced interventions that merely nudge the flow of events towards desired outcomes with minimal effort and disruption.

Within the strategic change literature, incremental and 'emergent' approaches are discussed that challenge the dominant disruptive orthodoxy (e.g. Mintzberg and Waters, 1985; Orlikowski, 1996; Feldman, 2000; Weick, 2009). Through 'Long March' (Kanter et al., 1992) or 'Theory O' (Beer and Nohria, 2000) approaches to change, disruptive strategic actions such as downsizing, layoffs or divestments are eschewed in favour of a coherent, incremental developmental process. Strategic change is alternatively imagined as a continuous, open-ended and iterative process of incrementally aligning and realigning organisational priorities with an ever-changing environment (Mintzberg and Westley, 1992; Weick and Quinn, 1999; Pettigrew et al., 2001; Falconer, 2002; Dawson, 2003). This process is colourfully described by Weick (2000: 225) thus: 'autonomous initiatives that bubble up internally; continuous emergent change; steady learning from both failure and success ... innovations that are unplanned, unforeseen and unexpected; and small actions that have surprisingly large consequences'.

Proponents of this emergent approach to strategic change display a greater awareness of how organisational actors, immersed in situations, act and respond to the immediacy of demands through purposive coping in situ guided by shared practices to effect incremental changes. By examining how practices are drawn on to iteratively fashioned novel but effective coping responses in situ, a processual outlook points to the potential of this less spectacular and disruptive approach to strategic change. Such an emergent approach describes well the case of the Development Bank of Singapore (DBS)

ILLUSTRATIVE EXAMPLE: EMERGENT STRATEGIC CHANGE IN DBS

DBS is a Singapore-based, multinational banking and financial services group serving millions of retail customers and institutional clients worldwide. As a consequence of decades of successful activity, DBS's modus operandi is characterised by continual strategic renewal around digital technologies. Sia et al. (2021) trace this history through phases in which 'nimble' enterprise architecture was developed: core digital, mobile and internet banking capabilities were nurtured, and an entrepreneurial mindset encouraged as the norm – such as to 'create a 26,000-person start-up' based on everyday practices of agility, customer-focus, experimentation and risk-taking. DBS now employ more software engineers than bankers, and use technology giants such as Google and Apple as points of competitive reference.

The cumulative impact of these historical paths has been the emergence of ambidexterity and dynamic capability in DBS. This gradual process of growing internal DC is used to capitalise on external exigencies and to, more recently, defy the apparent gravity of Covid-related challenges. As summarised in their annual report (DBS, 2022), DBS generated turnover of 14.3bn SGD and a net profit of 6.8bn SGD in 2021, up 44 per cent on 2020. The report highlights that when naming DBS as the 'World's Best Bank 2021', Euromoney commented that DBS has been 'not just surviving a [global pandemic] crisis but using it as a chance to innovate and to be a better bank. As well as fortitude and profitability, it showed opportunism and smart thinking, all underpinned by its digital leadership'.

From its position of strength, DBS remains as committed as ever to continual renewal. The DBS annual report for 2021 highlights a need to transform services to 'make banking joyful' for its customers. It remains at the forefront of technology, promotes ethical investing and sustainability, adopts flexible work practices in line with post-pandemic employee expectations and improves social contributions and impact. In playing down recent successes, DBS public statements promise, with humility, to keep 'looking further out, given that technological changes could fundamentally reshape the financial system, we must do what we can to be ahead of the curve' (DBS, 2022: 9).

Observational Fidelity: Beginning with the Senses to Effect Change

Experiences of active or passive resistance from stakeholders, of withdrawal of cooperation from staff, of pretend acceptance, and of unintended consequences are commonplace responses to strategic change initiated from above. Much of the wasted effort, energy and potential for improvement is avoidable by attuning the senses to latent sentiments, benign concerns, and suppressed anxieties denied expression across stakeholder groups. Through immersion in everyday practices and the nurturing of relationships, the capacity for discriminative attunement to subtle changes in attitudes, behaviour and predisposition displayed by and among organisational members can be nurtured.

Jullien (2011) observes that much of changes in life take place through 'silent transformations'. They often happen gradually and imperceptibly like the process of aging or the steady erosion of a riverbank. Likewise, the building up of strong and lasting human relationships, for example, does not happen quickly or all at once. Instead, it is gradually strengthened over time through numerous iterative interactions; the determined facing down of challenges, the mutual compromises made, the ongoing figuring out and making of minute adjustments and the overcoming of small resistances. This is how confidence, trust and tolerance of the other is built. Similarly, it is through this sort of continual flow and interplay of everyday happenings that bottom-up strategic change incubates and is realised. Awareness of such naturally occurring silent transformations leads to the realisation of the need to hone and refine our observational sensitivities.

Observational fidelity underpins the capacity for discriminative attunement and hence the accurate reading of actual goings-on in the world. Fidelity in observing derives from a disciplined adherence to 'artistic rigour' (Ehrenzweig, 1967: 29). Unlike scientific rigour which is usually equated with 'thoroughness and precision ... care and comprehensiveness in ... the gathering of extensive empirical evidence ... and logical soundness and justification in terms of the claims being made' (Chia, 2014: 684), artistic rigour entails the striving to attain an 'uncompromising democracy' of vision associated with the 'purity' of seeing. This emphasis on pristine and even 'child-like' seeing and sensing is highly valued and emphasised in the arts and in Oriental thinking.

For example, the poet William Wordsworth in *Expostulation and Reply* (1798/1967: 17) coined the term 'wise passiveness' to describe observational fidelity as 'a state of calm, contemplative receptivity' that allows 'the body to absorb the impulses from the external world and be enlightened by it' (in Chia, 2014: 672). Likewise, the art critic and social reformer John Ruskin insisted that the ability to see 'purely' – an 'innocence of the eye' (Ruskin, 1927, in Chia and Holt, 2007: 516) – is a prerequisite for performative excellence. Artistic rigour, wise passiveness and the innocence of the eye all allude to the importance of observational fidelity as a prerequisite for effective action and hence strategic change interventions.

This same emphasis on pure seeing is found in the writings of Zen-inspired legendary Japanese industrialists Konusuke Matsushita (2002) and Kazuo Inamori (2014). In their management philosophies, both insisted on the need for nurturing a '*sunao*' (observationally meek, humble, innocent, tractable) seeing to aid effective strategic decision-making. 'The untrapped, open mind – *sunao* – is a temperament that allows one to see things as they really are ... We have made it a regular management policy at Matsushita Electric to cultivate this *sunao* mind, in the conviction that it enables us to perceive the real state of all things in society' (Matsushita, 2002: 45). A crucial enabler of effective strategic change is this observational fidelity and the discriminative attunement that derives from it. This emphasis on relying fundamentally on the senses rather than the intellect to establish what is needed and to then respond accordingly is a consequence of embracing a processual worldview.

ILLUSTRATIVE EXAMPLE: THE UBIQUITOUS CATTLE GRID

The cattle grid provides an example of how a simple but effective solution can be developed from cultivating observational fidelity and an associated capacity for discriminative attunement. Cattle grids are ubiquitous on rural roads and tracks in the proximity of cattle and sheep farms. They comprise a set of metal bars spaced apart and placed over a hole in the road. The metal grids allow humans and vehicles to cross, but not sheep or cattle, or any four-legged animal for that matter. Cattle grids prevent farm animals from straying out of a particular farm territory or grazing patch, effectively serving as 'invisible gates'.

But how have they become so widely used as a means of restricting cattle and sheep movements by farmers? The answer lies in the observational fidelity and discriminative attunement of farmers, leading to a crucial insight about the fundamental difference between how humans and animals walk. Animals have great difficulty in coordinating the movement of four legs with the same agility as bipedal humans, impeding their successful negotiation of the gaps in the cattle grid. Animals attempting to cross invariably get trapped by the cattle grid, requiring to be helped out. Over time, cattle and sheep learn to avoid even attempting to cross these cattle grids, thereby rendering the grids highly effective but unobtrusive 'gates' that prevent the animals from straying.

Cattle grids are a simple device that help farmers manage their livestock in an inconspicuous and efficient way. Fashioned from a valuable insight arising from keenness of observation of the difference between how humans and animals coordinate their leg movements when walking, cattle grids are an example of the power of observational fidelity.

Rethinking Strategic Change: The Silent Efficacy of Oblique, Circuitous Action

We have examined the value in nurturing and attaining a level of observational fidelity in guiding strategic change responses to the processual flow and momentum of reality. Like a surfer subtly adjusting their board to ride a wave, we noted the inherent efficiency of making timely, targeted small insertions, informed by a refined discriminative attunement, to nudge the relentless flows of change towards desired outcomes. Natural changes are skilfully mobilised to advantage unobtrusively and without fuss; interventions are inevitably inconspicuous and oftentimes unnoticed by the untrained eye. Change then appears as an unexceptional part of the natural propensity of things to those involved in it. It is not jarring, does not attract undue attention and hence does not generate any unnecessary anxiety. Internal harmony is maintained and resisting forces minimised.

From this approach arises an appreciation that many sustainable achievements are attained quietly, indirectly and circuitously (Chia, 2014). Obliquity and circuitousness are concepts that allude to the staying power of indirect actions that deliver favourable outcomes without fanfare (Chia and Holt, 2009). Oblique actions create the perception that favourable outcomes are seemingly the inevitable consequence of the natural flow of events. Rather than relying on direct, brute force to effect outcomes, to some degree in opposition with naturally occurring flows, obliquity and circuitousness of approach tap into ongoing unowned change processes to produce the desired effect. Such obliquity of intervention is key to realising sustainable strategic change in a world that is itself relentlessly changing.

The effectiveness of oblique action is intimated in the economist and Financial Times columnist John Kay's (2010) observation that the richest people did not set out to deliberately accumulate wealth, the most profitable corporations are not those obsessively 'profit-driven', and the happiest people do not deliberately seek happiness. It seems that lasting achievements are oftentimes attained obliquely or circuitously, happening quietly in an understated manner rather than via dramatic, heroic action. But because such oblique insertions tend to be diffused and discreet, they are also inevitably less noticed and hence less appreciated by those seeking the spectacular and sensational. Yet, there is every reason to believe in the strategic efficacy of such indirect action (Chia and Holt, 2009). Celebrating the seemingly passive, understated and circuitous as opposed to the spectacular, dramatic and disruptive, is what differentiates a genuinely processual approach to strategic change from that typically championed in the strategic change literature

A processual worldview intimates the deep appreciation that with time, seemingly innocuous changes occurring in situ and at localised levels can eventually result in larger-scale dramatic transformations. This insight is expressed in ancient truisms, both West and East – 'Large streams from little fountains flow, Tall oaks from little acorns grow' or 'A journey of a thousand miles begins with the first step'. These truisms allude to a recurring awareness of the transformative power of small, seemingly insignificant initiations. They remind us not to be too beguiled by the dramatic and the spectacular.

From such a processual perspective, strategic change arises from continual iterative adjustment of collective organisational practices in situ, oftentimes obliquely and circuitously. This indirect approach to strategic change importantly shifts attention away from one-off dramatic interventions to the cumulative impact of seemingly innocuous everyday coping actions and decisions taken across the organisation. Appreciating this framing of strategic change demands a greater contextual awareness, and a heightened sensitivity to the internal 'propensity of things' (Jullien, 1999) always already going on. Strategic advantage awaits those able to exploit this key insight.

Conclusion: Elevating Strategy-in-Practices

an opportunity is simply the end result of an evolution and has been prepared by the duration of that evolution. So, far from coming about unexpectedly, it is the fruit of an evolution that must be taken in hand as soon as it begins or as soon as it is discernible

(Jullien, 2004: 65).

In this Element, we have articulated an alternative agenda for organisational strategy-making by drawing on a processual worldview to show that strategic tendency is always already contained in an organisation's shared practices. Shared organisational practices provide the kind of patterned consistency of actions that enable us to recognise the inadvertent emergence of strategy post-hoc. We call this strategic potential immanent in shared organisational practices SiP. *Strategy-in-Practices* points to strategy-making as an ongoing activity that manifests itself in effective everyday practical coping actions taken by organisational members independent of any formalised strategic planning process. SiP explains how the inadvertent emergence of an unplanned strategy is possible.

This process-practices perspective to organisational strategy-making is underpinned by the 'practice turn' in social theory which views practices as the founding basis of the regularities and improvisations that shape and define the conduct of everyday social life. A process worldview thus intimates the central and crucial role sociocultural practices and operational coping actions play in the creation of social structures, orders and patterned regularities that make up societies and organisations. From a process-practices understanding of social phenomena, practices are the 'building blocks' of these social entities. A processual worldview, therefore, posits that these social entities, including organisations, are no more than stabilised and congealed 'bundles' of shared practices containing patterned regularities of interactions. Likewise, 'the environment', 'markets' and even 'strategy' are similarly bundles of such practices.

Practices themselves are, in turn, shaped by inherited sociocultural tendencies and by the historical aggregation of a multitude of in situ everyday practical coping actions that have proven effective and served the collective over time. These coping actions are taken purposively 'on the hoof' rather than purposefully. They are 'goal-seeking' and are often driven by the need to alleviate us from an undesirable situation faced or to capitalise or take advantage of an available affordance immediately detected, rather than 'goal-driven' and intended to fulfil any pre-defined set of objectives. Purposive practical coping actions are essentially prospective in character and the success of these coping actions ensures the continued application of such practices so that a patterned consistency of response eventually ensues.

The aggregation and congealing of a whole multitude of everyday practical coping actions taken by organisational members, guided by sociocultural tendencies and acquired operational know how, produces collectively shared organisational practices containing consistencies and patterned regularities that we call an organisation's modus operandi. Modus operandi is the main source of patterned consistency in the 'stream of actions and decisions' that enables Mintzberg (1978) to justify his notion of 'emergent strategy'. Without this modus operandi contained in a strategic impulse that we call SiP, unplanned emergent strategy would not be possible. Our coining of SiP alerts us to strategy-making activities always already going on in an organisation at all levels even though there may be little evidence of any planned strategy. This explains why some successful organisations appear 'strategy-less'.

Effective practical coping actions, in turn, rely fundamentally on an observational fidelity to actual goings-on in the world for detecting what an extant situation affords to the actor immersed in it. It implies the cultivation of a discriminative attunement to situational affordances; the ability to differentiate between fine differences that intimate potential opportunities for advantage-gaining moves. As such, the perception of situational/environmental affordances depends upon on how finely tuned the discriminative capacity is in an organisation. Cultivated discriminative attunement coupled with the internalised modus operandi contained in shared organisational practices provide the micro-foundations for the dynamic capabilities of an organisation (Nayak et al., 2019), underpinning the 'sensing', 'seizing' and 'transforming' capacities articulated by Teece (2012). On this basis, we argue that dynamic capabilities are shaped by tacitly acquired sensitivities and in situ responsiveness rather than routines, rules or heuristics. In this way, SiP supports Teece's assertion that dynamic capabilities are idiosyncratic and historically shaped whilst offering explanations of how dynamic capabilities arise from the creative evolution of practices over time and in context.

A process-practices perspective also intimates a fundamentally different approach to initiating strategic change. Instead of the intermittent, episodic and oftentimes 'heroic' approach to strategic change promoted by the mainstream literature, it redirects attention to iterative, incremental and ongoing 'nudging' adjustments as the more appropriate basis for successful change interventions. Such an approach eschews the direct, dramatic and spectacular in favour of the indirect, oblique and circuitous; drawing from ancient wisdoms that remind us that transformations often begin with small seemingly innocuous gestures rather than grand initiatives. A process-practices perspective privileges the multitude of small, seemingly endless coping adjustments as the proper basis of sustainable change initiatives. But privileging these minute ongoing adjustments means, yet again, a reliance on a nurtured sensitivity to operational realities at 'ground' level. Observational fidelity nurtured through 'artistic rigour' produces the kind of disciplined, pristine seeing that is needed for detecting 'differences that make a difference' to the effectiveness of any change initiative. This refined capacity for discriminative attunement is what determines the likely success of a process-practices approach to strategic change.

Acquiring information by detecting fine differences through the senses (importantly though not to be associated with feelings or emotions) and not through the intellect, allows us to assess what is actually going on and hence to forge appropriate responses to the situation faced. But how can we best attune ourselves to our environment and allow the sensory inputs to apprise us of the situation confronted? In some way, our sensing actions begin with the 'education of attention'; with actively noticing fine changes and differences arising in our context and the affordances they potentially proffer. The prerequisite, however, is an intense and extended immersion oftentimes within mundane operational contexts, such as spending time at the coalface of production or service provision.

This immersion is of necessity, of an exploratory nature. It is 'purposeless' scanning that facilitates the noticing of things and events otherwise overlooked. This is how Ratan Tata, the founder of India's Tata Corporation, caught up in the daily grind of traffic congestion and in a moment of unguarded 'mind wander', was able to notice for the first time something he saw on a daily basis; a single scooter carrying an entire family with father driving it. This unguarded attention-drawing moment alerted him to an unarticulated need and gave him the inspiration to design and launch the Nano, the world's smallest car (Chacko et al., 2010) with great success!

The typically unconscious digestion of such perceptual insights helps refine our capacities to read, interrogate and interpretate our context for opportunities to bootstrap ourselves and creatively realise advantages. In short, the capacity for pristine 'innocent' seeing is a foundational prerequisite for discoveries, inventions and innovation. Like the flight of an aeroplane, it must begin from the ground of concrete observation before it can rise up into the 'thin air' of 'imaginative generalisation' in order to forge genuinely novel solutions (Whitehead, 1929/1978: 5).

Informed by a cultivated discriminative attunement, our coping actions are guided towards seizing advantage often through subtle, nuanced and oblique gestures rather than directly, dramatically and confrontationally. This is not a scattergun approach. Rather it is about the astute selecting and attending to of those aspects of an unfolding reality that appear promising and that offer possibilities for extracting sustainable benefit. Through timeliness of intervention, the flow of reality is effectively mobilised to work in our favour much like the way we might wait for the season and weather for planting seeds that eventually grow to yield a crop of beneficial outcomes. Further, our actions are sustainable precisely because they are respectful and in harmony with the natural order of things.

This processual approach to seizing entails a built-in flexibility for adaptation that enables appropriate response to the solicitations and affordances proffered from moment to moment. Through willingness to 'pilot' rather than 'navigate' from each unique situation to another, it becomes more possible to maximise the potential of circumstances encountered. To some extent, sensing, seizing and transforming implies detecting, grasping, reconfiguring and reframing of our understanding of the world. It entails embedding new practices – exploiting potential through collaborative innovation and reinforcing social gains through building new, or revising existing, social structures and orders. The result of heightened sensitivity to environmental affordances and a well-honed capacity for taking advantage of such affordances proffered, is ultimately a conservation of energy and an economy of effort involved: maximal gain for minimal expenditure of effort and energy. This is what makes for civilisational and hence organisational progress (Sahlins and Service, 1960).

Time and again in mainstream approaches to strategy and strategy-making, disappointing outcomes of the deliberate strategic planning approach evoke a doubling down on further refining of conceptual methods within the existing substantialist worldview. Such actions cannot possibly address the root cause of the failure. Practitioners and researchers devise ever more sophisticated, calculative technologies to sharpen logical arguments and abstractions of the dynamics of the world in hope rather than expectation of improving the effectiveness of strategy-making. New language and concepts package up revised substantialist practices that disguise enduring intractable issues and that replicate *ad nauseam* the Whiteheadian 'Fallacy of Misplaced Concreteness'.

By prioritising the primacy of the senses over intellect as a crucial starting point for understanding the world and remixing the influence of observational and conceptual orders in strategy, we are more likely to recover the true value of technologies, abstractions and logic as essentially supplementary and complementary to the potential and momentum of in situ creative coping practices. In this regard, SiP is an attempt to shift priorities away from the intellect to the senses, from thought to coping action and from planned to emergent in situ strategy-making. In embracing this processual approach in dealing with the world of human affairs we can restore a greater sense of usefulness and practicality to the concept of strategy in practitioner and academic circles.

References

Adolph, K. E., & Kretch, K. S. (2015). Gibson's theory of perceptual learning. In J. D. Wright (Ed.), *International Encyclopedia of the Social & Behavioral Sciences* (2nd ed., pp. 127–34). Amsterdam: Elsevier.

Analis, A. (2012). Commerce international – tell me a story – Francisco Trapani, CEO of Bulgari. www.youtube.com/watch?v=WA1vHeMOHqQ (accessed 23 April 2022).

Ansoff, H. I. (1975). Managing strategic surprise by response to weak signals. *California Management Review*, 18, 21–33.

Aristotle (1933). *Metaphysics, Vol. 1: Books 1–9* (H. Tredennick, Trans.). Cambridge, MA: Harvard University Press.

Aristotle (1998). *The Metaphysics* (H. Lawson-Tancred, Trans.). London: Penguin Books.

Ashcroft, J. (2014). Interview: The man who rescued Lego. www.youtube.com/watch?v=JlVyiFqIg0w (accessed 21 August 2022).

Barnes, B. (2001). Practice as collective action. In T. R. Schatzki, K. Knorr Cetina, & E. von Savigny (Eds.), *The Practice Turn in Contemporary Theory* (pp. 17–28). London: Routledge.

Barney, J. (1991). Firm resources and sustained competitive advantage. *Journal of Management*, 17(1), 99–120.

Bateson, G. (1972). *Steps to an Ecology of Mind*. New York: Chandler.

Beer, M., & Nohria, N. (Eds.) (2000). *Breaking the Code of Change*. Boston, MA: Harvard Business School Press.

Bennis, W., & O'Toole, J. O. (2005). How business schools lost their way. *Harvard Business Review*, 83(5), 98–104.

Bergson, H. (1903/1955). *An Introduction to Metaphysics*. Englewood Cliffs, NJ: Prentice Hall.

Bergson, H. (1911/1998). *Creative Evolution*. London: Macmillan.

Bergson, H. (1946/1992). *The Creative Mind*. New York: Carol.

Bohm, D. (1980). *Wholeness and the Implicate Order*. London: Routledge.

Bourdieu, P. (1977). *Outline of a Theory of Practice*. Cambridge: Cambridge University Press.

Bourdieu, P. (1990). *The Logic of Practice*. Stanford, CA: Stanford University Press.

Bourgeois, L. J., & Eisenhardt, K. M. (1988). Strategic decision processes in high velocity environments: Four cases in the microcomputer industry. *Management Science*, 34(7), 816–35.

Brownlee, J. (2016). The man behind Ikea's world-conquering flat-pack design. https://fastcompany.com/3057837/the-man-behind-ikeas-world-conquering-flat-pack-design (accessed 12 May 2022).

Burgelman, R. A., Floyd, S. W., Laamanen, T. et al. (2018). Strategy processes and practices: Dialogues and intersections. *Strategic Management Journal*, 39(3), 531–58.

Burgelman, R. A., & Grove, A. S. (2007). Let chaos reign, then rein in chaos – repeatedly: Managing strategic dynamics for corporate longevity. *Strategic Management Journal*, 28(10), 965–79.

Burns, R. (1786). *Poems, Chiefly in the Scottish Dialect* (1st ed.). Kilmarnock: John Wilson.

Burt, G., Mackay, D. J., van der Heijden, K., & Verheijdt, C. (2017). Openness disposition: Readiness characteristics that influence participant benefits from scenario planning as strategic conversation. *Technological Forecasting and Social Change*, 124, 16–25.

Chacko, P., Noronha, C., & Agrawal, S. (2010). *Small Wonder: The Making of the Nano*. New Delhi: Westland.

Chia, R. (1996). *Organizational Analysis as Deconstructive Practice*. Berlin: de Gruyter.

Chia, R. (1998). From complexity science to complex thinking: Organization as simple location. *Organization*, 5(3), 341–69.

Chia, R. (1999). A 'rhizomic' model of organizational change and transformation: Perspective from a metaphysics of change. *British Journal of Management*, 10(3), 209–27.

Chia, R. (2004). Strategy-as-practice: Reflections on the research agenda. *European Management Review*, 1(1), 29–34.

Chia, R. (2014). Reflections: In praise of silent transformation – allowing change through 'letting happen'. *Journal of Change Management*, 14(1), 8–27.

Chia, R., & Holt, R. (2007). Wisdom as learned ignorance: Integrating east-west perspectives. In E. H. Kessler & J. R. Bailey (Eds.), *Handbook of Organizational and Managerial Wisdom* (pp. 505–26). Thousand Oaks, CA: Sage.

Chia, R. C. H., & Holt, R. (2009). *Strategy without Design: The Silent Efficacy of Indirect Action*. Cambridge: Cambridge University Press.

Cooper, R. (1976). The open field. *Human Relations*, 29(11), 999–1017.

Dawson, P. (2003). *Organizational Change: A Processual Approach*. London: Routledge.

Day, G. S. (2007). Is it real? Can we win? Is it worth doing? *Harvard Business Review*, 85(12), 110–20.

DBS (2022). DBS annual report 2021. www.dbs.com/iwov-resources/images/investors/annual-report/dbs-annual-report-2021.pdf (accessed 4 June 2022).

De Saussure, F. (1966). *Course in General Linguistics*. New York: McGraw Hill.

Deleuze, G. and F. Guattari (1988). A Thousand Plateaus (trans. B. Massumi). Athlone Press, London.

Denning, S. (2014). Why IBM is in decline. www.forbes.com/sites/stevedenning/2014/05/30/why-ibm-is-in-decline (accessed 22 August 2022).

Detienne, M., & Vernant, J.-P. (1978). *Cunning Intelligence in Greek Culture and Society*. Chicago: University of Chicago Press.

Dreyfus, H. L. (1991). *Being-in-the-World*. Cambridge, MA: MIT Press.

Dreyfus, H. L. (2002). Intelligence without representation: Merleau-Ponty's critique of mental representation the relevance of phenomenology to scientific explanation. *Phenomenology and the Cognitive Sciences*, 1(4), 367–83.

Dunne, J. (1997). *Back to the Rough Ground: Practical Judgement and the Lure of Technique*. Notre Dame, IN: University of Notre Dame Press.

Ehrenzweig, A. (1967). *The Hidden Order of Art: A Study in the Psychology of Artistic Imagination*. London: Weidenfeld & Nicolson.

Eisenhardt, K. M., & Martin, J. A. (2000). Dynamic capabilities: What are they? *Strategic Management Journal*, 21(10/11), 1105–1121.

Falconer, J. (2002). Emergence happens! Misguided paradigms regarding organizational change and the role of complexity and patterns in the change landscape. *Emergence*, 4(1/2), 117–30.

Fehrenbach, P. (2014). IBM ditches 'roadmap': Workers say good riddance. www.industryweek.com/archived-team-play/article/22011409/ibm-ditches-roadmap-workers-say-good-riddance (accessed 22 August 2022).

Feldman, M. (2000). Organizational routines as a source of continuous change. *Organization Science*, 11(6), 611–29.

Ferguson, A. (1767/1966). *An Essay on the History of Civil Society* (D. Forbes, Ed.). Edinburgh: Edinburgh University Press.

Flyvbjerg, B. (1998). *Rationality and Power: Democracy in Practice*. Chicago, IL: University of Chicago Press.

Ford, J. D., & Ford, L. W. (1994). Logics of identity, contradiction, and attraction in change. *Academy of Management Review*, 19(4), 756–85.

Gersick, C. J. (1991). Revolutionary change theories: A multilevel exploration of the punctuated equilibrium paradigm. *Academy of Management Review*, 16, 10–36.

Ghemawat, P. (1986). Sustainable advantage. *Harvard Business Review*, 64(5), 53–8.

Gibson, J. J. (1950). The implications of learning theory for social psychology. In J. G. Miller (Ed.), *Experiments in Social Process: A Symposium on Social Psychology* (pp. 149–67). New York: McGraw-Hill.

Gibson, J. J. (1979). *The Ecological Approach to Visual Perception* (Classic ed.). New York: Psychology Press.

Gibson, E. J. (1982). The concept of affordances in development: The renascence of functionalism. In W. A. Collins (Ed.), *The Concept of Development: The Minnesota Symposia on Child Psychology* (Vol. 15, pp. 55–81). Hillsdale, NJ: Lawrence Erlbaum Associates.

Gibson, J. J. (1986). *The Ecological Approach to Visual Perception*. Boston, MA: Houghton Mifflin.

Gibson, E. J. (1988). Exploratory behavior in the development of perceiving, acting, and the acquiring of knowledge. *Annual Review of Psychology*, 39, 1–41.

Gibson, E. J. (1992). How to think about perceptual learning: Twenty-five years later. In H. L. Pick, P. van den Broek, & D. C. Knill (Eds.), *Cognition: Conceptual and Methodological Issues* (pp. 215–37). Washington, DC: American Psychological Association.

Gibson, E. J. (1997). An ecological psychologist's prolegomena for perceptual development: A functional approach. In C. Dent-Read & P. Zukow-Goldring (Eds.), *Evolving Explanations of Development: Ecological Approaches to Organism-Environment Systems* (pp. 23–45). Washington, DC: American Psychological Association.

Gibson, J. J., & Gibson, E. J. (1955). Perceptual learning: Differentiation or enrichment? *Psychological Review*, 62(1), 32–41.

Gould, S. J., & Vrba, E. S. (1982). Exaptation: A missing term in the science of form. *Paleobiology*, 8(1), 4–15.

Havelock, E. A. (1976). *Origins of Western Literacy: Four Lectures Delivered at the Ontario Institute for Studies in Education, Toronto, March 25, 26, 27, 28, 1974*. Michigan: University of Michigan.

Havelock, E. A. (1982). *The Literate Revolution in Greece and Its Cultural Consequences*. Princeton, New Jersey: Princeton University Press.

Heidegger, M. (1971). *On the Way to Language*. New York: Harper & Row.

Hernes, T. (2014). *A Process Theory of Organization*. London: Oxford University Press.

Hitt, M. (1998). Twenty-first-century organizations: Business firms, business schools, and the academy. *Academy of Management Review*, 23, 218–24.

Inamori, K. (2014). *Amoeba Management: The Dynamic Management System for Rapid Market Response*. New York: Productivity Press.

Ingold, T. (2000). *The Perception of the Environment: Essays on Livelihood, Dwelling and Skill*. London: Routledge.

Ingold, T. (2011). *Being Alive: Essays on Movement, Knowledge and Description*. London: Routledge.

Inkpen, A., & Choudhury, N. (1995). The seeking of strategy where it is not: Towards a theory of strategy change. *Strategic Management Journal*, 16(4), 313–32.

James, W. (1909/1996). *A Pluralistic Universe*. Lincoln, NE: University of Nebraska Press.

James, W. (1911/1996). *Some Problems of Philosophy*. Lincoln, NE: University of Nebraska Press.

Jarrett, M., & Huy, Q. N. (2018). Leadership: IKEA's success can't be attributed to one charismatic leader. *Harvard Business Review Digital Articles*, 1–5.

Jarzabkowski, P. (2008). Shaping strategy as a structuration process. *Academy of Management Journal*, 51, 621–50.

Johnson, G., Melin, L., & Whittington, R. (2003). Guest editor's introduction: Micro strategy and strategizing: Towards an activity-based view. *Journal of Management Studies*, 40(1), 3–22.

Johnson, G., Scholes, K. (1997). *Exploring Corporate Strategy* (4th ed.). London: Prentice Hall.

Jones, G. (2012). The growth opportunity that lies next door. *Harvard Business Review*, 90(7/8), 141–5.

Jullien, F. (1999). *The Propensity of Things: Towards a History of Efficacy in China*. New York: Zone Books.

Jullien, F. (2000). *Detour and Access: Strategies of Meaning in China and Greece* (S. Hawkes, Trans.). Princeton, New Jersey: Zone Books.

Jullien, F. (2004). *A Treatise on Efficacy: Between Western and Chinese Thinking* (J. Lloyd, Trans.). Hawai'i: University of Hawai'i Press.

Jullien, F. (2011). *The Silent Transformations* (K. Fijalkowski & M. Richardson, Trans., 1st ed.). London: Seagull Books.

Kanter, R. M., Stein, B. A., & Jick, T. D. (1992). *The Challenge of Organizational Change*. New York: Free Press.

Kay, J. (2010). *Obliquity: Why Our Goals are Best Achieved Indirectly*. London: Profile Books.

Kierkegaard, S. (1843). *Journalen* JJ: 167.

Koffka, K. (1935). *Principles of Gestalt Psychology*. New York: Harcourt Brace.

Kohtamäki, M., Whittington, R., Vaara, E., & Rabetino, R. (2022). Making connections: Harnessing the diversity of strategy-as-practice research. *International Journal of Management Reviews*, 24(2), 210–232. https://doi.org/10.1111/ijmr.12274.

Krupnik, I., Aporta, C., Gearheard, S., Laidler, G. J., & Holm, L. K. (2010). *SIKU: Knowing Our Ice*. New York: Springer.

Langley, A. N. N., Smallman, C., Tsoukas, H., & Van de Ven, A. H. (2013). Process studies of change in organization and management: Unveiling temporality, activity and flow. *Academy of Management Journal*, 56(1), 1–13.

Langley, A., & Tsoukas, H. (2016). *The SAGE Handbook of Process Organization Studies*. London: Sage.

Lewin, K. (1951). *Field Theory in Social Science*. New York: Harper & Row.

Little, J. (1996). *The Warrior Within: The Philosophies of Bruce Lee*. New York: Chartwell Books.

Mackay, D., Arevuo, M., & Meadows, M. & Mackay, B. (2023). *Strategy: Theory, Practice, Implementation* (2nd ed.). Oxford: Oxford University Press.

MacKay, B., Chia, R., & Nair, A. K. (2021). Strategy-in-practices: A process philosophical approach to understanding strategy emergence and organizational outcomes. *Human Relations*, 74(9), 1337–69.

Mackay, D., & Zundel, M. (2017). Recovering the divide: A review of strategy and tactics in business and management. *International Journal of Management Reviews*, 19(2), 175–94.

Mackay, D., Zundel, M., & Alkirwi, M. (2014). Exploring the practical wisdom of mētis for management learning. *Management Learning*, 45(4), 418–36.

MacKenzie, N. G., Perchard, A., Mackay, D., & Burt, G. (2022). Unlocking dynamic capabilities in the Scotch whisky industry, 1945–present. *Business History*, 1–21. https://doi.org/10.1080/00076791.2022.2085251.

Mansley-Robinson, J. (1968). *An Introduction to Early Greek Philosophy*. Boston, MA: Houghton Mifflin.

March, J. G. (1972). Model bias in social action. *Review of Educational Research*, 42(4), 413–29.

March, J. G. (2003). A scholar's quest. *Journal of Management Inquiry*, 12(3), 205–7.

Marx, K. (1852). *The Eighteenth Brumaire of Louis Bonaparte*. New York: Die Revolution.

Maturana, H., & Várela, F. (1980). *Autopoiesis and Cognition: The Realisation of the Living*. Dordrecht: D. Reidel.

Matsushita, K. (1978/1986). *My Management Philosophy* (National Productivity Board, Singapore, Trans.). Tokyo: PHP Institute.

Matsushita, K. (2002). *The Heart of Management*. New York: PHP Institute.

McLuhan, M. (1962). *The Gutenberg Galaxy*. Toronto: University of Toronto Press.

McLuhan, M., & Logan, R. K. (1977). Alphabet, mother of invention. *Et Cetera*, 34, 373–83.

McLuhan, M., & McLuhan, E. (1988). *The Laws of Media: The New Science*. Toronto: University of Toronto Press.

Merleau-Ponty, M. (1962). *Phenomenology of Perception*. London: Routledge.

Merleau-Ponty, M. (1963). *The Structure of Behavior* (A. Fisher, Trans.). Boston, MA: Beacon Press.

Merton, R. (1936). The unanticipated consequences of purposive social action. *American Sociological Review*, 1, 894–904.

Miller, D. (2003). An asymmetry-based view of advantage: Towards an attainable sustainability. *Strategic Management Journal*, 24(10), 961–76.

Mintzberg, H. (1973). *The Nature of Managerial Work*. New York: Harper & Row.

Mintzberg, H. (1978). Patterns in strategy formation. *Management Science*, 24(9), 934–48.

Mintzberg, H. (2004). *Managers, Not MBAs*. Harlow: Financial Times Prentice Hall.

Mintzberg, H., & Waters, J. A. (1985). Of strategies, deliberate and emergent. *Strategic Management Journal*, 6(3), 257–72.

Mintzberg, H., & Westley, F. (1992). Cycles of organizational change. *Strategic Management Journal*, 13, 39–59.

Nayak, A., Chia, R., & Canales, J. I. (2019). Noncognitive microfoundations: Understanding dynamic capabilities as idiosyncratically refined sensitivities and predispositions. *Academy of Management Review*, 45(2), 280–303.

Ong, W. J. (1967). *The Presence of the Word*. New Haven, CT: Yale University Press.

Ong, W. J. (1982). *Orality and Literacy: The Technologizing of the Word*. London: Routledge.

O'Reilly III, C. A., Harreld, J. B., & Tushman, M. L. (2009). Organizational ambidexterity: IBM and emerging business opportunities. *California Management Review*, 51(4), 75–99.

O'Reilly III, C. A., Tushman, M. (2008). Ambidexterity as a dynamic capability: Resolving the innovator's dilemma. *Research in Organizational Behavior*, 28, 185–206.

Orlikowski, W. J. (1996). Improvising organizational transformation over time: A situated change perspective. *Information Systems Research*, 7(1), 63–92.

Peteraf, M. (1993). The cornerstones of competitive advantage: A resource-based view. *Strategic Management Journal*, 14(3), 179–91.

Peteraf, M., Di Stefano, G., & Verona, G. (2013). The elephant in the room of dynamic capabilities: Bringing two diverging conversations together. *Strategic Management Journal*, 34(12), 1389–410.

Peters, T. (1989). *Thriving on Chaos*. London: Pan.

Peters, T. J., & Waterman, R. H., Jr. (1984). *In Search of Excellence: Lessons from America's Best-Run Companies*. New York: Harper & Row.

Pettigrew, A. (1973). *The Politics of Organisational Decision-Making*. London: Tavistock.

Pettigrew, A. (1992). On studying managerial elites. *Strategic Management Journal*, 13, 163–82.

Pettigrew, A. M. (2012). Context and action in the transformation of the firm: A reprise. *Journal of Management Studies*, 49(7), 1304–28.

Pettigrew, A. M., Woodman, R. W., & Cameron, K. S. (2001). Studying organizational change and development: Challenges for future research. *Academy of Management Journal*, 44(4), 697–713.

Pfeffer, J., & Fong, C. (2002). The end of business schools? Less success than meets the eye. *Academy of Management Learning and Education*, 1, 78–95.

Polanyi, M. (1966). *The Tacit Dimension*. New York: Doubleday.

Porter, M. E. (1980). *Competitive Strategy*. New York: Free Press.

Porter, M. E. (1984). *Competitive Advantage: Creating and Sustaining Superior Performance*. New York: Free Press.

Prigogine, L. (1989). The philosophy of instability. *Futures*, 21, 396–400.

Rescher, N. (1996). *Process Metaphysics*. New York: State University of New York Press.

Romanelli, E., & Tushman, M. (1994). Organizational transformation as punctuated equilibrium: An empirical test. *Academy of Management Journal*, 37, 1141–66.

Ruskin, J. (1927). *The Complete Works*. London: Weidenfeld & Nicolson.

Sahlins, M. D., & Service, E. R. (1960). *Evolution and Culture*. Ann Arbor, MI: University of Michigan Press.

Sanders, J. T. (1993). Merleau-Ponty, Gibson and the materiality of meaning. *Man and World*, 26(3), 287–302.

Schatzki, T. (2001). Introduction: Practice theory. In T. Schatzki, K. Cetina, & E. Savigny (Eds.), *The Practice Turn in Contemporary Theory* (pp. 1–14). London: Routledge.

Schatzki, T. R., Cetina, K. K., & von Savigny, E. (2001). *The Practice Turn in Contemporary Theory*. Routledge.

Schatzki, T. R. (2005). The sites of organizations. *Organization Studies*, 26(3), 465–84.

Schonberger, R. (1982). *Japanese Manufacturing Techniques: Nine Hidden Lessons in Simplicity*. New York: Free Press.

Scott, J. C. (1998). *Seeing Like a State: How Certain Schemes to Improve the Human Condition Have Failed*. New Haven, Connecticut: Yale University Press.

Shingo, S. (1985). *A Revolution in Manufacturing: The SMED System*. New York: Productivity Press.

Sia, S. K., Weill, P., & Zhang, N. (2021). Designing a future-ready enterprise: The digital transformation of DBS bank. *California Management Review*, 63(3), 35–57.

Smith, B. (2021). Red ventures has turned very specific advice into very big business. www.nytimes.com/2021/08/15/business/media/red-ventures-digital-media.html (accessed 21 August 2021).

Spender, J.-C. (1989). *Industry Recipes: An Inquiry into the Nature and Sources of Managerial Judgement.* Oxford: Blackwell.

Starkey, K., & Tempest, S. (2009). The winter of our discontent: The design challenge for business schools. *Academy of Management Learning & Education*, 8, 576–86.

Taleb, N. (2013). *Antifragile: Things that Gain from Disorder.* London: Penguin Books.

Teece, D. J. (2007). Explicating dynamic capabilities: The nature and micro-foundations of (sustainable) enterprise performance. *Strategic Management Journal*, 28(13), 1319–50.

Teece, D. J. (2012). Dynamic capabilities: Routines versus entrepreneurial action. *Journal of Management Studies*, 49(8), 1395–401.

Teece, D. J. (2014). The foundations of enterprise performance: Dynamic and ordinary capabilities in an (economic) theory of firms. *Academy of Management Perspectives*, 28(4), 328–52.

Teece, D. J., Pisano, G., & Shuen, A. (1997). Dynamic capabilities and strategic management. *Strategic Management Journal*, 18(7), 509–33.

Torczyner, H. (1977). *Magritte: Ideas and Images.* New York: Harry N. Adams.

Tsoukas, H., & Chia, R. (2002). On organizational becoming: Rethinking organizational change. *Organization Science*, 13(5), 567–82.

Van de Ven, A. H. (1987). Review essay: Four requirements for processual analysis. In A. M. Pettigrew (Ed.), *The Management of Strategic Change* (pp. 326–341). Oxford: Blackwell.

Van de Ven, A. H., & Poole, M. S. (1995). Explaining development and change in organizations. *Academy of Management Review*, 20, 510–40.

von Mises, L. (1949/1998). *Human Action: A Treatise on Economics* (Scholar's ed.). Auburn, AL: Ludwig von Mises Institute.

Weick, K. E. (1979). *The Social Psychology of Organizing* (2nd ed.). Reading, MA: Addison-Wesley.

Weick, K. E. (2000). Emergent change as a universal in organisations. In M. Beer & N. Nohria (Eds.), *Breaking the Code of Change* (pp. 223–41). Boston, MA: Harvard Business School Press.

Weick, K. E. (2009). *Making Sense of the Organization: The Impermanent Organization.* West Sussex: John Wiley.

Weick, K. E., & Quinn, R. E. (1999). Organizational change and development. *Annual Review of Psychology*, 50, 361–86.

Wernerfelt, B. (1984). A resource-based view of the firm. *Strategic Management Journal*, 5(2), 171–80.

Whitehead, A. (1926/1985). *Science and the Modern World*. London: Free Association Books.

Whitehead, A. N. (1929/1978). *Process and Reality*. New York: Free Press.

Whitehead, A. N. (1933). *Adventures of Ideas*. New York: Macmillan.

Whittington, R. (1996). Strategy as practice. *Long Range Planning*, 29(5), 731–5.

Whittington, R. (2002). The work of strategizing and organizing: For a practice perspective. *Strategic Organization*, 1(1), 119–27.

Whittington, R. (2019). *Opening Strategy*. Oxford: Oxford University Press.

Winter, S. G. (2003). Understanding dynamic capabilities. *Strategic Management Journal*, 24(10), 991–5.

Wordsworth, W., & Coleridge, S. T. (1798/1967). Expostulation and reply. In W. J. B. Owen (Ed.), *Lyrical Ballads* (Vol. 1, pp. 17–24). London: Methuen.

Zeng, J., & Mackay, D. (2019). The influence of managerial attention on the deployment of dynamic capability: A case study of Internet platform firms in China. *Industrial and Corporate Change*, 28(5), 1173–92.

Zollo, M., & Winter, S. G. (2002). Deliberate learning and the evolution of dynamic capabilities. *Organization Science*, 13(3), 339–51.

About the Series

Business strategy's reach is vast, and important too since wherever there is business activity there is strategizing. As a field, strategy has a long history from medieval and colonial times to today's developed and developing economies. This series offers a place for interesting and illuminating research including industry and corporate studies, strategizing in service industries, the arts, the public sector, and the new forms of Internet-based commerce. It also covers today's expanding gamut of analytic techniques.

Cambridge Elements ☰

Business Strategy

Elements in the Series

A full series listing is available at: www.cambridge.org/EBUS

Printed in the USA
CPSIA information can be obtained
at www.ICGtesting.com
LVHW021240240823
756042LV00001B/82